Our History
My Testimony

THE HEZEKIAH DILLAHUNT STORY

Anointed Press
PUBLISHERS

Cheltenham, MD
www.anointedpresspublishers.com

Our History
My Testimony

THE HEZEKIAH DILLAHUNT STORY

Hezekiah Dillahunt Sr.

Our History My Testimony - The Hezekiah Dillahunt Story

Hezekiah Dillahunt, Sr. (c) 2015

ISBN 13: 978-0-9860790-6-1

Disclaimer Clause

To purchase additional books:

hezekiahdillahunt@gmail.com
www.anointedpresspublishers.com
www.amazon.com

Internal Layout:
Nicole Morgan

Cover Design:
Starvin Artists

Published by:
Anointed Press Publishers
(a subsidiary of Anointed Press Graphics, Inc.)
11191 Crain Highway
Cheltenham, MD 20623
301-782-2285

IN MEMORY OF MY WONDERFUL WIFE,
EUNICE DILLAHUNT

Without you, I would not have been able to write this book.
Though you are not with me on earth, you are forever in my
heart, my thoughts, and my memories.

January 5, 1930 – December 28, 2021

Acknowledgements

First and foremost, I thank God for giving me the inspiration to write this book, and for the leading and guiding of the Holy Spirit.

I am greatly indebted to my Pastor, Rev. Dr. Lee P. Washington who provided insight and encouragement throughout the process.

I thank my wife, Eunice, and my children: Derek, Cassandra, Michelle and Hezekiah Jr., for allowing me to fulfill God's will for my life.

Thanks to Wanda L. Scott who transcribed my thoughts from tape to manuscript.

Many thanks to Sheila Anderson, Esq. , who gave of her time and expertise in working toward getting the book compiled.

I also thank my bowling partners and friends who gave me encouragement and monetary gifts to help speed up the publication process.

TABLE OF CONTENTS

1

1920-1929

In America, the years between 1920-1929 were affectionately known as the *Roaring 20's.* According to the Census Bureau, the population was about 107 million. Of that 107 million people, an estimated 2 million were unemployed, 5.2%. The life expectancy of males and females was 53.6 and 54.6, respectively. Down from the 1,172,601 reported in 1919, there were only 343,000 people in the military. The average annual income was $1,236. On the bottom side of that average, much like today, the average salary for a teacher was $970. The 1920's were an especially important time in the life of African Americans. Not too far removed from the oppression of slavery, abolished only 55 years prior, it is in this decade that the Lord allowed African Americans to begin moving into the center of this stage called the United States of America.

The Ku Klux Klan was one of the fastest growing racist organizations known to man. It operated in over twenty-seven states in America. Its membership, well over 100,000 in 1920, operated mostly in the South and motivated Blacks to migrate to the North. By the year 1920, the population of African Americans had nearly doubled in the northern cities of Chicago, St. Louis, New York, Philadelphia, Indianapolis, Washington DC, Cleveland, Detroit, Pittsburgh, and Boston. Blacks left to pursue a fear-free life and opportunities in areas not easily afforded to them. Those that remained in the South were mainly employed as farmers and sharecroppers.

The Arts and entertainment industry was the area where African Americans were most recognized in the 1920's. It was the decade when music, art, theater, and literature came alive in a movement called the Harlem Renaissance; aptly named because of its origin in Harlem, New York. Also called the Negro Movement, the Harlem Renaissance is best known for changing the way that Blacks were viewed in America. No longer were they just ex-slaves, they were tearing down the doors in the world of creative arts, showing that African Americans were both intellectual and creative.

At the end of 1920, Broadway opened its doors to the first all Black cast in a jazz-musical called "Shuffle Along" with Eubie Blake, and Florence Mill. Later, Paul Robeson and Josephine Baker would join the cast.

In 1924, Opera star Roland Hayes, became the first African American to perform a full recital at Carnegie Hall in New York City. In the dance world in 1925, Josephine Baker could be spotted dazzling audiences in Paris, France with an American jazz production entitled *La Revue Negre.*

Back in the United States, the Savoy Ballroom and the Cotton Club were the two most famous arenas for performers and dance groups in the 1920's. Though the Cotton Club was "Whites only" until 1927, when Edward Kennedy "Duke" Ellington made his debut, it was forever changed. The two dance halls were where dances such as the "Lindy Hop" became famous.

The 1920's saw landmark achievements in the world of literature for African Americans as well. In 1923, *The Opportunity Magazine: Journal of Negro Life* began its publication under the editorship of Dr. Charles Johnson. The magazine became an influential outlet for the published works of African American writers, especially during the Harlem Renaissance. On its heels, in 1925, Dr. Alain LeRoy Locke published *The New Negro*. It was an anthology of essays and other writings about the role African Americans played in developing American culture. It detailed achievements in art, music and

5

literature as well as speculations about the future of African Americans.

Inspired by the lack of a medium for Blacks to express the conditions associated with Black life in the South, W.A. Scott II, in 1928, launched his own newspaper to educate, inspire, uplift and promote the expression of the Southern Black Community.

There were two very noteworthy individuals in the fields of Architecture and Design during that era. In 1926, Paul Revere Williams, known as the 'architect to the stars' because of the numerous homes that he designed for celebrities, became the first African American accepted as a fellow in the American Institute of Architects. His achievements paved the way for Henry Ossawa Turner to become the first African American artist elected to the National Academy of Design in 1927.

In a time when the annual salary of America was $1,200, Garret Morgan, inventor of the traffic light, earned $40,000 when he sold its patent to General Electric in November 1923.

The 1920's were a time of significant achievements in the lives of African American female scholars as well. In 1921, Eva B. Dykes, Sadi T. Mossell, and Georgiana R. Simpson became the first African American women to earn Ph. D's in English, Economics and German philology, respectively.

The following year, Bessie Coleman, known as 'Queen Bess', became the first female African American pilot. Having been rejected by all American flight schools, Coleman obtained her pilots' license in only seven months from the Caudron Brothers' School of Aviation in Le Crotoy, France. She was the first Black woman in the world to receive an aviation license.

Paving the way for now President Barack Obama, the National Bar Association, made up of mostly African American attorneys was established on August 1, 1925 in Des Moines, Iowa.

As a part of his research for the Association of Negro Life and History in 1926, Carter G. Woodson established Black History Week as a means to pay tribute to the significant achievements of African Americans. In 1976, Black History Week officially became Black History Month.

The 1920's yielded some pretty big firsts for African Americans in the sports world also. Not to be excluded from America's favorite pastime of baseball, in 1922 the New York Renaissance were formed by Robert Douglas from Harlem, NY. They would become the first professional all-Black baseball team and the predecessors for athletes like Jackie Robinson, Satchel Paige and Barry Bonds.

Two years later, in 1924 a twenty-one year old track star from the University of Michigan, William DeHart Hubbard, would travel to the Games of the VIII Olympiad to become the first African American to win an individual gold medal in the long jump.

At the same time that Blacks in the North were singing the Blues and dancing to the tunes of Bessie Smith and the Duke, in the backwoods of Pollocksville, NC, there was another type of dancing going on. It was a celebratory dance that took place in the hearts of my parents, Lemuel and Joanna Dillahunt, to announce my birth on July 22, 1924. And so my story begins...

I was the 10th of 17 children. We lived in a four-bedroom home in the country– the *real* country, in the woods in North Carolina. Pollocksville is a small town in Jones County, North Carolina, only 0.3 square miles. My Uncle Aurelius and his wife Cora lived in our neck of the woods. They owned quite a few acres of land and had a lot of children, so there was always a lot of fun when we were together.

Our family was poor. As a child, I remember hearing the scripture about Jesus coming to the poor and wondered if that was why my father prayed so often. He was a farmer and we grew our own food. We raised cows, chickens, hogs, and ducks, and we grew any other food that we were able to get to grow. My mother was a homemaker and the jewel of my life. She would spend her days making sure that we were all clean, fed and taken care of.

I was five years old when the United States Stock Market collapsed. That was the day that we would all come to know as 'Black Tuesday.' I was too young to remember the specifics of the collapse, but I would soon get an idea of what the first Great Depression was all about.

2 1930-1939

In the summer of 1930, I turned six years old. I remember walking to school four miles one way. We didn't have any streetcars or an automobile of our own. In order to get to school, we had to cross three ponds just to get to the road that led to the school. Whenever there was a large rainstorm the ponds would flood and we'd have to wade, knee-deep, through them. But they say that necessity is the mother of invention. That was certainly the case with our family.

My father grew tired of us coming home from school sick as a result of being in wet clothes all day. We knew that the city was not going to build a bridge or anything like that for the Black kids living in the country to get to school, so my father made one.

He was so skillful. He got his tools out and cut down a few large trees. He put gashes in them that we could use for foot-holds and no longer did we have to walk in water to get to school. My father's love was like the love of the Lord. He would never let us struggle for too long before he built a bridge over troubled water. He was a good provider.

The Depression was especially hard on Blacks that were struggling even before the Stock Market crash of 1929, like my family. I give all praise to God for keeping us through that time.

Just as the Lord used my father's skill to provide for and make our family better, He's used people in all different walks of life and their skills to make the world a better place. The first area that comes to mind is in the world of sports.

The day after my birthday, on July 23rd, one of my biggest icons, Josh Gibson, became the catcher for the Pittsburgh Homestead Grays. His nickname was the 'Black Babe Ruth.'

I've been told that for hoboes, hopping freight cars were popular pastimes in the Depression years- especially in 1931. For some, it seemed to create a sense of adventure in the dreariness of their daily lives. Perhaps it was a search for adventure that brought the nine young black men that we would soon know as the "Scottsboro Nine" out where trouble would find them. While hopping freight trains, the men had a run in with a White, female passenger and the end result was that they were arrested and accused of raping her. The case entered the courts on April 6, 1931 and due to false evidence and a lack of due process, it went all the way to the Supreme Court.

Living in the backwoods, we had limited access to radio signals so we were always late getting the news. But when the people where I lived finally did get the news about the trial, they were all up in arms–and rightfully so. The trial ended with their convictions being overturned in

1937. It was a landmark case because it was the first time that a defendant's right to an attorney was brought to the Supreme Court. I remember that! The Lord showed favor on them and just as we, as a community, were up in arms about their convictions, we celebrated, as a community, when they went free.

The Scottsboro Boys were riding on a freight car when their troubles ensued. While some young people were relegated to only moving from train to train to pass their time, in other areas of the United States, Blacks were making big moves in different ways.

In the area of Black life, the Nation of Islam was established by the Honorable Elijah Muhammed in Detroit, Michigan.

In arts and entertainment, Edward Kennedy Ellington, more commonly known as "Duke", produced one of his most popular tunes, the smooth sound of *Mood Indigo.*

With a literary contribution, *Black Bourgeoisie,* that would become required reading for many University students, in 1931 Dr. E. Franklin Frazier published his book, *The Free Negro Family.*

In 1932, President Franklin D. Roosevelt was elected into office. He, like President Obama, came into office at a time when the United States was in dire financial straits. He was elected to a platform that included something called "The New Deal." Simply put, it was a series of ideas and programs designed to get America back on its feet after the Depression. The following year I would get firsthand knowledge of how the Depression was really affecting my family and why the New Deal was so important.

In 1933, as part of the New Deal, President Roosevelt established an agency called the CCC, Civilian Conservation Corps. It was a work-relief program for young men from unemployed families whose job was primarily to conserve the natural resources of the country–timber, soil and water. It was to provide training and employment for the duration of the Depression.

There were a few stipulations that came with working in the CCC. You had to be between 18-26, unmarried and a U.S. citizen. My brother fit the qualifications and went off to work with them. The regulations must have been monitored loosely because I remember my father going to work for them as well. My father and brother would get up at about three in the morning to get dressed and pack their food. They had to walk for two miles to wait for a big truck that would come and take them and the rest of the workers to the job site. In the winter, they'd put a tin heater on the truck to stay warm. You could see the smoke stack piping out of the side of the truck as they drove off.

Men that worked at the camps were paid $30 per month with mandatory $25 checks sent to the families. It may not sound like much now but it was enough to get us through in those days.

In the same year that the CCC was established, Roosevelt made other breaking news by both electing Mary McLeod Bethune to be one of the advisors in the President's "Black Cabinet", and inviting Etta Moten to sing at the White House. She would become the first African American stage and screen star to sing and perform there.

Another major event that took place in 1933 was the addition of the 21st Amendment to the Constitution. The amendment was added so that Prohibition could be repealed in December of 1933. Selling alcohol was the only way that some people could make money. There was a man named Jack Banks that lived near us and had a home-made distillery that he kept between our house and his. Back then, and especially where I lived, they didn't have any liquor stores, ABC stores or anything like that. So, people like Mr. Banks made big money selling their "hooch."

My grandmother kept liquor in her medicine cabinet. When we were sick she would give us what she called "life ever-lasting tea." She would mix the liquor with black coffee. It would be really strong and really black! She would give

17

us that concoction if we had a persistent cough. The next morning we'd be healed. That stuff knocked all manner of sickness out of you!

In 1934, I was ten years old and already working to help my family on the farm. My father and brother were working away from home, so my brothers and I did what we could do to pitch in. I went to school only about 3 months out of the year. The rest of the time I was working. And while I was working, there were some other Blacks in America that were working too.

Arthur W. Mitchell became the first African American Democrat elected to Congress. He won by defeating Oscar DePriest, a Republican from Illinois.

Dorothy West became the editor of the magazine, *Challenge*. The daughter of an emancipated slave, Ms. West was an integral figure during the years of the Harlem Renaissance and to President Hoover's Administration as one of the writer's for his WPA, Works Progress Administration.

Roy Wilkins took on an editor position also, for the NAACP's *Crisis* Magazine.

Still the platform by which many singers' careers are launched, in 1934 the Apollo Theater in Harlem, NY had its first live stage show. While the Apollo was setting up for its first big show, Louise Beavers was commanding audiences on the big screen. Though stereotypically typecast as a maid, or a "mammy," Ms. Beavers' role in *Imitation of Life* is noteworthy because it was the first time in cinema history that a Black woman's problems were given any emotional weight in a major Hollywood film.

In 1935 the National Council of Negro Women was established by Mary McLeod Bethune. She is best known for starting a school for Blacks in Daytona Beach, FL that would later become the Bethune-Cookman University. She was also an advisor to President Roosevelt during his Works Progress Administration. It was a program like the CCC that gave work to unemployed Blacks. My father also worked for the WPA before the war broke out.

The WPA program built many public buildings and roads. It operated large arts, drama, media and literacy projects. Today, almost every community in America has a park, bridge or school constructed by this agency. In 1939, it was renamed the Works Projects Administration, but whatever it was called, my father was proud to work and able to provide for his family.

Whenever my father wasn't away working and we could get a clear signal, he, my brothers and I, would sit around the house and listen to the radio. On one of those occasions we were lucky enough to be a part of history when we heard that Joe Louis, the *Brown Bomber,* had knocked out the former boxing heavyweight champion, Primo Carnera, in six rounds.

While we sat around singing the praises of Joe Louis, the New York Times was heralding that Marian Anderson was "one of the greatest singers of our times" after a Town Hall performance in 1935.

The year 1935 yielded the birth of someone for whom I still thank God for today, Dr. Percy Julian. He was a research chemist who developed a drug called physostigmine. It is used in the treatment of glaucoma; something that I am all too familiar with.

Some years later I would suffer with glaucoma to the degree that I was almost totally blind in one eye. I had surgery and began to take this medicine and things were much better. I give all thanks and honor to God for how he used a man, a Black man, the grandson of a slave, to develop this drug.

One of the reasons that I am writing this book is to show our young people that there is a genius that lies within all of us. The successes of the people in this book are in the past but they have laid a foundation for the successes that our young people can have in the future. There are people who are waiting on you to develop the next drug that will change their lives, like Dr. Julian did for me.

The year 1936 yielded another honor for Mary McLeod Bethune. On June 24th of that year, she became the first African American woman to receive a federal appointment by becoming the Director of Negro Affairs of the National Youth Administration.

A great accomplishment in the field of arts/entertainment was that of William Grant Stills. In 1936, he became the first African American given the honor of conducting a major symphonic orchestra. He was the guest conductor of the Los Angeles Symphony Orchestra at the Hollywood Bowl.

Shattering any fantasies in the mind of Hitler and anyone else that deemed Blacks an inferior race, in sports, Jesse Owens won four gold medals in track and field events at the 1936 Olympics in Berlin, Germany.

Paving the way for people like Supreme Court Justice Clarence Thomas, in 1937 William

H. Hastie became the first African American appointed a United States Federal Judge. He was appointed by President Roosevelt to the district court in the Virgin Islands.

In sports, Joe Louis bounced back on the scene as the Heavyweight Champion of the World when he defeated Jim J. Braddock on June 22, 1937.

Later in that year, the Brotherhood of Sleeping Car Porters became a full-fledged union under the leadership of Asa Philip Randolph on October 1, 1937. It was the first labor organization led by African Americans to receive a charter in the American Federation of Labor.

Labor is another area that I am all too familiar with. In 1937, I was still working on the farm and I remember a very funny story. I was about 12 or 13 years old and one of the white families who owned a plantation near us hired my brothers and me to weed out the grass growing near their crops. We were too far from home to go back for lunch, so we would go out among the pecan trees, lie on the grass and eat the lunch that we brought from home. We would take about a 2-hour break and try to get a nap in during that time. One day when our lunch was over the white lady and her brothers started pressuring us to see our penises. They chased us every day for about two weeks until I came up with a plan.

I told my brothers and some other guys that the farm owners hired to work with us, to drink plenty of water the morning before they came to work. I told them that when the white lady and her brothers tried to proposition us, that I would let them do what they wanted. I was going to let them look at it. I was wearing a pair of those old bibbed overalls that had a big gap in the front. I told the guys that when they pulled it out, it was going to be just as if they'd turned on a faucet to water their grass. And that's exactly what happened. When they came and opened up my overalls, I opened up. I sprayed them all over their faces; got myself and everything else wet. But after that, I had no more problems with them trying to see my private parts. I knew that was a dangerous thing to do in the time that we lived in, but I needed them to respect me.

Respect is what the men and women who came before me were trying to attain. I'll never forget that and I try to instill a sense of self-respect in all of the people, especially the young people that I come in contact with everyday.

In 1938 Marion Turner Stubbs founded the Jack and Jill America Center. It was something like today's YMCA; a program with a commitment to help develop educational, cultural, civic and social programs for the betterment of African American youth.

In law and politics, Crystal Bird Fauset became the first African American woman elected to a state legislature, and attorney, Thurgood Marshall, was appointed by the NAACP to Special Counsel for Legal Cases.

In Arts and entertainment, Benny Goodman, a white jazz clarinetist, withstood a great deal of controversy and protest for having an integrated band. He invited to play with him, Teddy Wilson on piano and Lionel Hampton on vibes.

Joe Louis retained his heavyweight championship status by knocking out the German fighter, Max Schmeling.

African American females in Arts and entertainment and politics had a great year in 1939.

Jane Bolin was named the first African American female judge. She was appointed to the Domestic Relations Court in New York City.

Hattie McDaniel made history in the movie industry. She became the first African American to win an Oscar as best supporting actress for her role as *Mammy* in *Gone with the Wind.*

Hoping to follow in her footsteps, Lena Horne graced the big screen for her first movie, *The Duke is Tops.*

Though praised by the New York Times just four years earlier, in 1939 Marian Anderson was denied the privilege of singing at Constitution Hall in Washington, DC on Feb. 27th. The Daughters of the American Revolution (DAR) had a "white artists only" policy up until the year 1952, but Ms. Anderson did sing there in 1943. Eleanor Roosevelt, First Lady at that time, resigned her membership when Marian Anderson was not allowed to sing at the hall.

3
1940-1949

The 1940's were dominated by World War II. European artists and intellectuals fled Hitler and the Holocaust, bringing new ideas to other parts of the world. War production pulled us out of the Great Depression. Women needed to replace men who had gone off to fight in the war, and so the first great exodus of women from the home to the workplace began.

The population was about 132,122,000. In the year 1940 there were roughly 8,120,000 people unemployed. The average salary was $1299. A teacher's salary was slightly higher at $1441. Up $.18 from its inception in 1938, the federal minimum wage was $.43/hour.

Fifty-five percent of U.S. homes now had indoor plumbing. Antarctica was discovered to be a continent. The life expectancy of males and females, respectively, were 60.8 and 68.2. The world was changing.

When 1940 rolled in, I was 15 and preparing to do something different with my life. I'd been working since I was 8 years old and it was making me into a good man. We would sometimes work from dawn to midnight all week long- except for Sundays. We didn't work on Sundays. We always took the Sabbath and went to church. But when we weren't at church I was working in the tobacco fields and it was rough. I'd say to myself, "Lord, if You ever let me get grown and leave this place, I'm going to make something of myself and I'm going to give You the glory." In a few years, He would do just that.

In the meantime, in the world of literature, Richard Wright was becoming an acclaimed author as his book, *Native Son,* was published. He became the first African American novelist to attain a Book of the Month Selection.

Benjamin O. Davis became the first African American United States military general with the rank of Brigadier General on October 16, 1940. I actually had a chance to meet him. His brigade was traveling through the town that I lived in and stopped to have one of their trucks serviced at the neighborhood store. We all had questions for him and when asked where he was going, he told us that he was in route from Camp David. He was in full uniform, complete with brass and medals and everything. It was really something!

Also in the field of military service, in 1941 Dorie Miller, a United States Navy man, was awarded the Navy Cross for heroism during the Japanese attack on Pearl Harbor. Years later, his life would be portrayed on film by the actor, Cuba Gooding, in the film "Pearl Harbor."

Partly in an effort to further dampen the stronghold of segregation in the US, and partly to ensure that there would be no strikes or demonstrations that would disrupt the manufacture of military supplies, President Roosevelt ordered an end to discrimination in all defense industries with Executive Order 8802 on the eve of World War II. The order opened up more jobs for African Americans.

The Tuskegee Institute was formed in 1940. I had a friend, Mr. Alfonso Brooks, who was one of the original Tuskegee Airmen. The formation of the institute was controversial because it would be the first program specifically designed for African American pilots. The institute would later be notorious for their clinical study involving 399 poor, mostly illiterate, African American sharecroppers. The subjects were studied to show the affects of syphilis if left untreated. The men were never given consent forms and were denied treatment when penicillin arrived in 1947 and became the standard treatment for syphilis.

Dr. Charles Drew, a professor of surgery at Howard University in Washington DC, established a method for blood banks that is used in America and Great Britain.

Booker T. Washington became the first African American to be honored on a stamp. It was proof positive that the racial climate in America really was changing. And just as things were changing in and for America, the Dillahunt household was changing too.

All of the children in my house were growing up. We were teenagers and young adults. My sisters started courting. Most of the boys lived on big plantations and they had cars. My sisters were beautiful and very shapely. The guys would take them out for rides and sometimes they would drive around to different church services. My father would tell them what time to be home and they obeyed.

More space was being created in the house because my sisters were getting married and moving out. My father decided to add more rooms to the house–a sitting room and a closed in porch. I was 16 or 17 and getting ready to move out myself but there were things that I still needed to learn. Driving was on that list.

My daddy bought a car and began to teach his boys how to drive. We didn't have money to put tires on the car every time we got a flat, so we spent a lot of time buying pumps and patches to fix the broken inner tubes. We learned how to make it work. My father taught us that.

I remember that my father would let my brother and I use the car to go see our girls. We, like our sisters, had a curfew but my brother never wanted to obey the rules. It seemed like he never knew how to get home on time. If I was at my girlfriend's house and it was nearing 9pm, I could almost hear my father saying, "As long as you stay under my roof, you're going to abide by my rules and regulations." My brother would stay at his girlfriend's house until 1am or sometimes later. It got to a point where when I couldn't get him to pick me up on time, I would start walking home. I remember several times walking home and just before I would get there, he would come whizzing around in the car. I'd be so angry. But there was nothing I could do because I was the youngest and he had the authority. He married one particular girl that he was seeing during that time.

One of my sisters, Emma Jane, married a guy named Godfrey Wiley. He was very mean to her after they started having children together. He started beating her. They didn't live too far from us, so when he'd hit her she would run to our house with the babies. One evening she'd been beaten so badly that my grandmother decided that some action needed to be taken. She didn't have a telephone to call the police or a car to drive to the station, so she decided to take matters into her own hands.

My daddy kept a loaded shotgun over the door. No one ever bothered it. Later, Godfrey came by the house to get my sister Emma Jane. My grandmother threatened to shoot him if he didn't stop abusing her. He was able to take the gun away from her. Shortly thereafter he and Emma Jane moved away. He was still beating her, but she wasn't close enough for us to get to her.

My father took a very hands-off approach about the situation. He looked at it like, "if she lets it happen, then I don't have anything to say." This was way before we started using terms like "domestic violence" or anything like that. I saw what my sister went through and I knew that I would never do anything like that when I got a wife.

I was taking all of these events in and learning from them. I knew that my time was soon coming to branch out into the world on my own, but I needed a little more development.

While I was looking to make changes in my life, there was a young group of college students looking to make a change in the world. CORE (Congress of Racial Equality) was founded in 1942 seeking change to racist attitudes in America. An interracial group, they were largely influenced by the non-violent resistance teachings of Mahatma Ghandi. CORE pioneered the tactics of sit-ins, jail-ins and freedom rides that would become the driving forces behind the Civil Rights Movement. In 1943, CORE staged its first sit-in protest against segregated restaurants at Jack Spratt's Coffee Shop on May 14th.

Another man that was destined to carve out his own path was self-taught engineer, Frederick McKinley Jones. In 1942 he invented and patented the refrigerator system used in automobiles, trucks, and railroad trains.

In politics, William L. Dawson was elected to the Unites States House of Representatives from Chicago. He was called the "Dean of Black Congressmen" after having served twenty-seven years.

In Arts and entertainment, Paul Robeson starred in the role of *Othello* on Broadway and set a record of 296 performances for a Shakespeare play.

The year 1943 yielded two big firsts for African Americans and the military. First, two American Navy Destroyer ships, the *USS Mason* and the submariner chase *PC1264,* were allowed to be staffed with African American navy men. Then, the 99th Pursuit Squadron flew in active combat. It was the first African American Army Corp unit sent out on a mission. The date was June 2, 1943.

January 5, 1943 brought about the end of life for the famed Tuskegee Scientist, Dr. George Washington Carver. Rising from slavery to become one of the world's most respected men, he is best known for developing crop-rotation methods for conserving nutrients in soil and discovering hundreds of new uses for crops such as the peanut.

In an attempt to become my own respectable man like Dr. Carver and my father, I chose to go back to school in 1943 when I turned

19. I hadn't gotten much further than the 8th grade and I didn't read well but I wanted to. I gave the Lord my life when I was 13 and I valued the relationship. My main goal was to be able to read and understand the Bible better. I stayed in school and studied for 2 years. Soon after that, I left the farm and moved out on my own.

Though I moved away from the farm, I was still working hard doing odd jobs. I was making $73.50 a week. Sometimes I would work overtime and make up to $100 more a week. After I paid my room and board, I would send $50 home to my family. I was saving to help my family move into a better home, outside of the backwoods. My father was 70 years old, and I wanted to see him in a better situation. He'd taken care of all of us his entire life and I wanted to do something for him in his old age.

World War II dominated most events between the years of 1939-45, yet there were still significant achievements to be celebrated as African Americans. One such achievement was that in 1944, we witnessed the election of Adam Clayton Powell, Jr. as the first person of African American descent elected to Congress from the Harlem, New York district.

While Powell was fighting for African Americans at home in the States, African American soldiers were fighting, for the first time, side by side with white American troops at the *Battle of the Bulge.* African Americans participated in record numbers in all branches of the armed services. Over three million registered to serve and preserve democracy around the world.

Just 66 years ago, in 1944, the United States Supreme Court ruled that white-only primaries, which excluded African Americans from voting, were unconstitutional.

In the fields of Arts/entertainment and publishing, 1945 was a big year for African Americans. It was in that year that Nat "King" Cole, the singer/pianist, became the first African American to have his own radio show. Eleven years later, he would host his own television variety show, becoming the first of our race to do that also. I remember listening to the Nat King Cole show.

Another singer, but in the field of opera, Todd Duncan, became the first African American to sing a leading role with an American opera company when he appeared in New York City's production of *II Pagliacci*.

Richard Wright published his well-received autobiographical novel, *Black Boy*. Chester Hines published his novel, *If He Hollers Let Him Go*. John Johnson published his most successful and widely circulated magazine, *Ebony*, in November of 1945 for the first time. It is still in publication today.

In sports, Jackie Robinson was on his way to the majors when he was picked by Branch Rickey to play with the Montreal Royals on August 28th. It was a step toward his playing for the Brooklyn Dodgers.

While all of that was going on, I was working and working on finding myself. I moved around from place to place and changed jobs a lot. Eventually, I wound up packing up my car and going back home.

While home, I ran into some of my friends. They knew that I'd been driving a truck hauling tires, pipes, water lines and other things. They were very curious about my travels and wanted to know if I belonged to the Masons. I didn't. They told me that they'd heard that being a Mason helped to protect Blacks when they were on the highway and got pulled over by the police. Belonging to the Masonry was supposed to be an invisible shield. I told them that I'd had an invisible shield all of my life in Jesus Christ. I told them that when I was in Sunday school as a child, I learned that if I put my trust in God that He would take care of me. And He did. I wasn't stopped for speeding one time while I was driving up and down the highways. I'd never been drunk and I'd never been to jail. In the end I told them that I didn't need the Masons because I had Jesus Christ.

I did odd jobs around town for a while and in the summer of 1945 I moved to Washington, DC to work. It was so incredibly different from my life in the South and I couldn't have picked a more tumultuous time to move. The country was getting ready to make a major shift and I was right in the center of all the action.

With the untimely death of FDR, 1945 ushered in a new president, Harry S. Truman. In his first year in office, in 1946, he appointed a National Committee on Civil Rights to study and investigate racial injustices in the United States.

In the field of law and politics, in the case of Morgan vs. Virginia, the United States Supreme Court ruled that segregation in interstate bus travel was unconstitutional.

Also in 1946, the American Nurses Association admitted African American nurses in the national chapter for the first time.

The following year, in sports, Jackie Robinson was making headlines again as he became the first African American to play for the major leagues. He officially became a Brooklyn Dodger on April 10, 1947.

Another powerful contribution to the literary world, Dr. John Hope Franklin published the first edition of *From Slavery to Freedom*.

The Congress of Racial Equality (CORE) tested the U.S. Supreme Courts outlaw of bus segregation by staging the first "Freedom Ride." The first riders were scheduled to start traveling April 9, 1947.

There are two reasons that 1948 was an important year for African Americans. The first was a bill from President Truman that outlawed lynching and the consequent creation of a Federal Commission of Civil Rights on February 2nd. The second was the signing of his Executive Order 9981, which called for an end to segregation and discrimination in the United States Armed Forces and all other areas of federal employment on July 26th. The racial climate was so hot that I'm sure these were not easy decisions for him to make. I know that the Lord had to be touching his heart. *The kings heart is in the hand of the Lord, as the rivers of water: he turneth it whithersoever he will. Proverbs 21:1(KJV).*

Dr. Ralph J. Bunche became the chief assistant to the United Nations, mediator in the Palestine crisis that ended the Arab-Israeli War in 1949. Two years later, in 1950, he would become the first African American to win the Nobel Peace Prize in connection with the Arab-Israeli cease-fire.

In sports, Alice Coachman became the first African American woman to win an Olympic gold medal. She was the only American woman to win the gold that year in London. Her area of expertise was the high jump.

A pioneer state, New Jersey, in 1949 became the first state to go on record as opposing discrimination in all public accommodations.

In arts and entertainment, leading the way for Howard and Cathy Hughes, WERD-AM became the first African American owned and operated radio station in the United States under the leadership and ownership of Jesse Blanton, Sr. in Atlanta, Georgia.

About 1,000 miles away in Annapolis, MD, Wesley A. Brown was celebrating his becoming the first African American to graduate from the United States Naval Academy.

In 1949, Jackie Robinson was named the MVP of the National Baseball League and I hit a home-run of my own. I was working in DC at a garage scrimping and saving all of the money that I could. At the end of the year, I was able to buy my family a house outside of the backwoods. I was really grateful to God that He'd allowed me to work and save up to do that for my family.

4

1950-1959

The population, according to the US
Department of Commerce, Bureau of the Census,
was approximately 151,684,000. Of that number,
a little over 15 million were African American,
approximately ten percent of the population.
There were about   3,288,000 people that were
unemployed. The life expectancy of women and
men were 71.1 and 65.6, respectively. There
were about 6, 665, 800 car sales and the average
salary was $2992. The ratio of men to women in
the labor force was 5:2, and the cost of a loaf of
bread was $.14 cents.

African Americans, in the years between
1950 and 1959, had a significant number of
achievements and moments that would continue

to shape the lives of future African Americans forever.

In April of 1950 we mourned the deaths of two great men, Dr. Carter G. Woodson and Dr. Charles Drew. Dr. Woodson was known as the "Father of Black History," and Dr. Charles Drew, the founder of American Blood Banks.

In Government, Edith Spurlock Simpson became the first African American to serve on the United States delegation to the United Nations.

Gwendolyn Brooks became the first African American to win a Pulitzer Prize for her volume of poetry entitled, *Annie Allen*. It was a very significant achievement for African Americans in literature as the Pulitzer is the highest literary award a person can attain.

In sports, Jackie Robinson became the first African American to appear on the cover of *Life* magazine. The Lord was allowing us to receive– not only recognition for our works–but public recognition and pay to go along with it. Magazine companies had to pay top dollar to feature someone of color on their front pages.

In 1951, Private First Class William Henry Thompson was posthumously awarded the Congressional Medal of Honor for bravery in the Korean War. He was the first enlisted man in the Korean War, and the first African American to receive the award since the Spanish-American War in 1898.

In July of 1951, the Unites States experienced one of its worst race riots to date. The aftermath of World War II saw a revival of white attacks on black mobility, mostly on the city's South and Southwest Sides, but also in the western industrial suburb of Cicero. Aspiring African American professionals desiring to obtain improved housing beyond the South Side ghetto, whether in private residences or in the new public housing developments constructed by the Chicago Housing Authority, were frequently greeted by attempted arsons, bombings, and angry white mobs often numbering into the thousands.

The 1951 Cicero riot lasted several nights and involved approximately two to five thousand white protesters, attracting worldwide condemnation. Between July 10th and 12th, thousands of White Cicero residents attacked an apartment building housing a single black family. Ultimately, 450 National Guardsmen and 200 Cicero and Cook County police officers were called in to control the fires, looting, and destruction. The media covered the Cicero riot and it became news across the United States and the world.

Joining the fight for equal treatment for Blacks, Mary Church Terrell, a civil rights activist, was able to convince the powers that be in Washington to outlaw segregation in all restaurants in the Nation's capitol. The final victory came on May 24, 1951.

On his way to becoming one of the most prominent figures in American history, Dr. Martin Luther King, Jr. graduated from Crozer Theological Seminary at the age of 22.

In government, Dr. Ralph J. Bunche was appointed Undersecretary of the Nations in December 1951.

When the door to 1952 opened, so was a door that had previously been closed in the face of African Americans. Opera singer, Dorothy Maynor, became the first African American to perform in the DAR Constitution Hall in Washington, DC. Only a few years earlier, singer Marian Anderson was refused an opportunity to perform there. The Lord was getting ready to bring about a change in the Nation and it started with the sound of music.

Also in the arts and entertainment field, Ralph Ellison published, *the Invisible Man.* In the following year, 1953, he became the first African American to win the National Book Award for this same book.

In law, for the first time in the United States, the Supreme Court agreed to hear the cases presented by the NAACP involving segregation in schools according to race.

In 1952, for the first time in 71 years, there were no recorded lynchings. That was wonderful news for Blacks but it is a shame that that was even something that needed to be celebrated.

From 1950-1952, I stayed at the house with my family. By the end of 1952, I'd gone back to farming for a couple years and the crops had finally begun to grow. We planted string beans and cucumbers. When they harvested, we took them to the market to sell. We also grew and sold tobacco. We had a good product. We were always offered excellent prices for our crops because we made sure that they always looked fresh. We'd sell the beans and other items for about $2-$3 per basket. I made out pretty well while farming for those 2 years back in North Carolina.

When 1953 rolled in, I prayed and believed that the Lord was leading me back to Washington, DC. I had been running into too many racist White people and I wanted a change of atmosphere, again.

I was making moves and other Blacks around the country were making major moves too. Still not out of the racist trenches, the 1950's was a politically unstable time for African Americans. Their rights were continually under attack. All the efforts made during the forties to integrate the Armed Forces were abolished during the Korean War. A new era of racist assassinations began to occur and African Americans started to take a stand against outright racism.

The NAACP argued cases in Southern states against discriminatory practices in the public school system. In May of 1954, Brown vs. Board of Education occurred. This landmark case ruled that racial segregation in public schools was unconstitutional. Chief Justice Earl Warren wrote the overriding decision and Thurgood Marshall led the legal defense team for the NAACP. The African American non-violent movement began taking the form of boycotts, sit-ins, and peaceful protests. The African American authors during this decade were writing about love, discrimination, the prison system, protest, black sexuality, and black life in Harlem.

Author, James Baldwin, became an overnight sensation with his first book, *Go tell it On the Mountain.*

The NAACP began a campaign called the "Fight for Freedom." It was to be a more aggressive model for fighting discrimination and segregation in America.

Baton Rouge, LA became the first city to boycott its segregated buses in June of 1953 and Earl Warren was appointed Chief Justice of the Supreme Court. During his tenure, there was much progress in moving the judicial system forward in the movement to eliminate racial barriers.

I had to start from scratch when I finally did make it back to DC. I found a job at a gasoline station on M Street. I was washing cars, changing oil, scrubbing driveways, and cleaning the restrooms. It was rough but I had to do it until something better came along.

In Arts and entertainment, actress Dorothy Dandridge starred in the movie, *Carmen Jones,* which won her an Oscar nomination for Best Actress.

In Sports, Willie Mays played for the NY Giants and his team won the pennant. He was voted the league MVP with a .345batting average.

A tune called *Progress* is what African Americans were humming in 1955. It was in that year that Marian Anderson was back in the headlines as she became the first African American to sing at the Metropolitan Opera House (the MET) in NYC. Ray Charles gained notoriety as his song, *I Got a Woman,* became a chart-topper. And, Chuck Berry's, *Maybellene,* hit the radio waves and set Blacks on a course that would establish them on the Rock & Roll circuit forever.

Just three years earlier we all rejoiced because it seemed like the days of Blacks being lynched was over. Then, on August 28, 1955, the body of Emmett Till was found in the river in Money, Mississippi. He'd been accused by the people that killed him of "whistling at a white woman." For that, his "punishment" was having his eye gouged out, being beaten beyond recognition, shot in the head and thrown into the Tallahatchie River with a 70 pound cotton gin fan tied to him with barbed wire. It was a sad time in American history. The main suspects were acquitted but later admitted to committing the crime.

The murder of Emmett Till was a major catalyst for the uprising of the American Civil Rights Movement, and also a major turning point in my life. Seeing someone so young, so brutally murdered for no reason made me decide instantly that I wanted to do something big with my life so that no man, White or otherwise, would feel like he could do anything like that to me.

In the area of Civil Rights, Roy Wilkins became the Executive Secretary of the NAACP.

His work, combined with the constant pressure from Blacks all around the Nation, pressured the United States Supreme Court to issue an order to desegregate all public schools "with deliberate speed."

It was in 1955 that Rosa Parks, as part of a planned political maneuver, refused to give up her seat on a segregated bus in Montgomery, Alabama. She was arrested. Four days later the Montgomery Improvement Association was organized and the famous bus boycott that lasted 381 days commenced. It was in this time that Dr. Martin Luther King Jr., having just received his Ph.D. in Systematic Theology from Boston University, was thrust into the forefront as the leader of the Civil Rights Movement. On December 21, 1956 the Supreme Court ruled that segregation on city bus lines was unconstitutional.

America was making strides and I was making strides, too! I was back in DC and had been working at a gas station. The Lord fixed it up to where I had an opening to leave that job and start working at the Fort Meade Navy Yard working on equipment. It was always very busy there and my job was to scrub the place so that it wouldn't ice over. It was a strenuous job but I stuck with it for as long as I could. When I'd had enough I went to see my sister who knew a man that owned a garage.

His name was Sherman and he owned a car dealership on P Street. My sister got him to agree to see me and he did. I went the next day and the Lord showed favor toward me. After we talked, the only thing I needed to do was give my current job two weeks notice and with that, I had a new job with Mr. Sherman at the dealership.

My job was pretty much to manage the body shop. There were so many cars on the road that there was plenty of work for people in the car repair business. The shop opened at 7 a.m. so I had to get up early in the morning to help put the cars on the stretchers, and drive them on the roof. There was parking on the roof of the building so that there could be space on the ground to work on them. I remember parking my car on the street and having to make a mad dash to move it by 4 p.m. so that I wouldn't get ticketed. But the Lord watched over me and I never was late to move it. I never received a ticket. But this job, too, would be short-lived.

Later on, in an attempt to make a little more money, I started working construction, a job I had worked years before. It just didn't seem to be working out. The money only minimally changed my paycheck—I needed more. I met a guy named Barry Fieldsburg. He was a salesman that I'd met when I was working at the Sunoco station. He'd opened up a gas station on the corner of Montana and Trinidad and asked me to come and work for him. He said that he knew I was an honest person who did good work and would never steal from him.

I didn't know right away that the Lord was setting me up, but He was. Barry needed a good service man and I needed insight into the business of running a station. I stayed there with Barry for a good while. It was long enough to give me time to go back to school and take up a course in automobile mechanics. I passed the course and received a certificate that stated that I was now a licensed mechanic. Things were looking up!

Things were looking up for African Americans all over, especially in the world of sports. In 1956, Althea Gibson became the first African American to win a major tennis title–the French Open Women's Single title. Milton Campbell became the first African American to win the gold medal for the decathlon at the Olympics. He'd taken home the bronze medal in the event in 1952.

In Arts/entertainment, Nat King Cole, who just a few years back was praised for being the first African American to host his own radio show, became the first African American to host a variety show. It was called, *the Nat King Cole Show.*

More than 1,000 school districts opened their doors for both African American and White children for the first time as integrated schools. There were still some states that didn't desegregate in 1956: North and South Carolina, Georgia, Virginia, Florida, Alabama, Mississippi and Louisiana.

The year 1957 was a huge year for Civil Rights in America. The first major civil rights legislation since 1875 came with the Civil Rights Act of 1957. It was a piece of legislation designed to protect voters and their right to vote. It was also in this year and time when the Southern Christian Leadership Conference was organized and Dr. Martin Luther King, Jr. was elected as president.

Making headlines in sports again, Althea Gibson won the singles title at the Wimbledon tennis championships in England.

Though the year had lots of highs for African Americans, 1957 marked one of my lowest years. It was the year that I lost my father. He'd been sick for a long time. We'd been battling for the past two years with insurance companies and welfare trying to get him the care and benefits that he needed. He was my hero. I learned how to be a man, and moreover, a man of God from Him. He taught me, and all of my brothers, to have work ethic. I was comforted in that I knew he knew the Lord, and that one day we'd meet on the other side. I knew that I just needed to keep living my life in a way that would make him proud of me. I pushed on.

While I pushed, Blacks in America pushed their way to higher heights as well.

When 1958 rolled in, it did so in a big way. Alvin Ailey stepped out into the limelight and began his famed dance company, the *Alvin Ailey Dance Theater* in NY.

Sidney Poitier became the first African American male to be nominated for Best Actor for his role in *The Defiant Ones.*

Dr. Martin Luther King Jr. was stabbed by a woman while signing copies of his book, *Stride Toward Freedom: the Montgomery Story,* in a

Harlem, NY bookstore. He was hospitalized but recovered.

The Civil Rights Act of 1957 was signed and put into action by President Dwight D. Eisenhower.

But of all the things that happened in Black life in the year 1958, none were more exciting than my nuptials to my wife of now 52 years, Mrs. Eunice Dillahunt, formerly McNeill. I met her when I was in my early 30's. We were introduced through a mutual friend and started dating. We spent as much time together as we could. I taught her how to drive and we traveled quite a bit, locally. Mostly we talked and went to church and that was right up my alley. I sang in the male chorus at Jerusalem Baptist Church. Sometimes she acted like she liked and wanted to be with me and sometimes she didn't, but I knew how I felt about her all along.

It was around Christmas and I was really busy but she'd asked if I could drive down to Fayetteville, North Carolina. She gave me her address and I made it my business to be there. When I arrived I met her parents and the rest of her family. It was during that trip I made my case as to why we should be together. We'd been dating on and off for about three and a half years. I told her that I didn't believe in spending too much time with a young lady unless I had intentions–and I did. Not too long after that we were married by Rev. Augustus Lewis and Rev. John Sattlewhite. Rev. Lewis was my pastor, and Rev. Sattlewhite was the Dean of Theological Studies at Livingstone College.

With my new wife came many new responsibilities, but I didn't back down from any of them. We were a young couple starting a new family but I didn't know that my marriage to Eunice was going to be the catalyst to changing my life forever. The Bible says, "Whoso findeth a wife findeth a good thing, and obtaineth favour of the LORD", (Proverbs 18:22) and I agree. My union with my wife definitely released a double portion of the Lord's favor on my life.

In 1959 we began to have children of our own. Derek was our first born son. I worked very hard to take care of my young wife and child.

While I was working hard, there were some other people working hard too. One of those people was Berry Gordy, Jr. In 1959, he started his own record company, Motown Record Corporation, in Detroit, MI. It grew into a multimillion dollar enterprise with stars such as Smokey Robinson, Marvin Gaye, Stevie Wonder, The Jackson Five, The Supremes, The Temptations and others.

On March 11th, Lorraine Hansberry opened her play, *A Raisin in the Sun,* starring Sidney Poitier. Less than a month later the play won the New York Drama Critics Circle Award for best play.

Another set of huge accomplishments in the Arts/entertainment field were Ella Fitzgerald and William "Count" Bessie winning Grammy

Awards. They were the first African Americans to ever do so.

On the heels of all of the good things that happened that year, there was a tragedy. A lynching was reported. Mack Charles Parker was hung in Poplarville, Mississippi for allegedly raping a white woman. Unfortunately, his murderers were never caught.

5

1960-1969

The years 1960-1969 were when the children from the post-war baby boom became teenagers and young adults. This was roughly 70 million children. There was a feeling amongst people to stray from the conservatism of the fifties and spread their wings in new, freer dimensions. There was a desire in the hearts of young people for change and they pushed until they saw them in the laws, education, values, entertainment and other social areas. Even in 2009, we can feel the residual effects of the groundwork that was laid during this decade.

Of a population of 177,830,000 people, 3,852,000 were unemployed. The National debt was $286.3B. The average salary was $4,743, with teachers making slightly more at $5,174. Minimum wage was $1. The life expectancy of males and females were 66.6 and 73.1, respectively. There were about 21.3 per 100,000 reported automobile related deaths.

There were significant Civil Rights incidents and achievements in the 1960's. The world was letting go of the reins of overt racism and segregation, really showing signs of moving toward a nation that is full of people who are more tolerant. President Eisenhower's term as president helped to put legislation in place to aid in the eradication of racism and segregation. In 1960, he signed into law a stronger, more aggressive and protective Civil Rights Act to deal with the disenfranchisement of Blacks seeking to register and vote.

The Student Non-Violent Coordinating Committee (SNCC) was organized and set up a nationwide network of student sit-ins. The first meeting was held at Shaw University, not too far from my hometown, in Raleigh, NC. Marion Barry was the organization's first national spokesperson. As a young person, I participated in various sit-ins. I was a Black man who was very familiar with being unfairly treated, especially in the South. I got involved because I wanted to feel like I was making a difference. Those sit-ins, combined with the help of the Lord, were very effective.

There was another sit-in movement that was put into place in February called, *Sit-Ins.* A few years into the 1960's when most Southern and border-states in America had segregated libraries, beaches, movie theaters, and restaurants, the Sit-Ins were fighting to make changes. The catalyst for this movement took place at a Woolworth's lunch counter by a group of North Carolina A&T University students in Greensboro, NC.

While some fought racism and inequality with sit-ins, there were some that took their silent protest to the field. In sports, Rafer Johnson carried the American flag at the Olympics. It was a first for an African American. And outdoing his 1956 silver, in 1960 he won the gold for the decathlon. Wilma Rudolph also had big wins during those Olympics. She gained national recognition when she won three Gold medals and was called the "World's Fastest Woman." The Associated Press named her the female athlete of the year for 1960.

Though making great strides, the road to the pathway of racial equality was filled with roadblocks and potholes. One of two such roadblocks was a riot that broke out on the University of Georgia's campus when two Black students, Charlayne Hunter and Hamilton Holmes, were admitted and enrolled into its previously segregated doors. The second was a test by CORE to test the new laws on transportation desegregation.

CORE was founded by a group of students on the campus of the University of Chicago. CORE still exists and its mission is to "bring about equality for all people regardless of race, creed, sex, age, disability, sexual orientation, religion or ethnic background. In pursuing its aim, CORE seeks to identify and expose acts of discrimination in the public and private sectors of society."

An integrated group of Freedom Riders got as far as Anniston, AL before they were beaten, and their Greyhound bus was burned.

In Arts/entertainment, Leontyne Price made her debut with the Metropolitan Opera Company in NY. She performed Verdi's, *Il Travatore*. On another end of the music spectrum, R&B Sensation, the Supremes, with Diana Ross, Mary Wilson and Florence Ballard made their first appearance as a group in Detroit, MI.

During this same time, Thurgood Marshall became Chief Counsel of the NAACP. In government, John F. Kennedy was then in office and appointed Thurgood Marshall to the Second Circuit Court of Appeals. Appointed by Lyndon B. Johnson, he became a Supreme Court Justice. He was the first African American to serve in this office.

In 1960, my family would undergo a major test. Before my father died, I bought my baby brother Thomas a car so that he could transport our father back and forth to doctor's appointments and other places that he needed to go. My first daughter, Valerie, was seven and living with my mother. She was having some problems getting into school because her birthday was after the deadline for enrollment, so most days she would just hang out around the house or outside in the yard. She'd been sitting outside, playing with matches, in or near Thomas' car. Her dress caught fire and she went running into the house screaming. Her clothes were singed and she was burned from her chest down. I then got the phone call that no father wants to hear. "Your daughter has been in a horrible accident."

I was living and working in Washington, DC (DC) at the time and she was in North Carolina. The staff at the hospital where she'd been taken told me that her injuries were severe and that they didn't have the facilities to take care of her properly. It was time to confer with God.

The Lord dropped the Children's Hospital on 13th Street in my spirit. I went there and told the doctors in the burn unit my situation. They told me that if I could get Valerie there, that they would do everything they could do to help her. I knew that I had to get her there, but if I put her in an ambulance from Trenton, NC to DC, it was going to cost more money than what I had. When I prayed and asked the Lord for wisdom, He gave me precise instructions about how I was supposed to transport Valerie. I was going to go get her and drive her back.

My sister, Ella, rode with me. When we got to the house, we cut the back seat out of my car and put a mattress in its place. I didn't want her to be any more uncomfortable than I already knew she would be. We put some sheets on the mattress and waited until the next morning to pick her up from the hospital in North Carolina. It was snowing very heavily, but I didn't care because all I could think about was getting my baby back to DC to get the care she needed.

When we got to the hospital, Valerie was wrapped from her breast to her waist in bandages. The doctors and nurses came in to give me all of the information they could about her situation. They wanted me to know how grim her situation was. I took in what they said, but I believed the report of the Lord. I knew that the Lord would heal my daughter and raise her up as He did Jairus' daughter (Mark 5:22). My faith in the Lord made me see Valerie whole and healed. I got her in the car and took her back to DC.

I took her to Children's Hospital. From the moment we got her there, they started working on her. She had third degree burns over three quarters of her body. The staff at Children's Hospital worked diligently on Valerie during her entire six month stay. She received over 16 skin grafts during her stay. I didn't have any money to pay her bills but the doctors had mercy on me. They told me that if I could just pay the hospital whatever I could, that the surgeons and other doctors would get their pay after she was well. I didn't pay anything until Valerie was out of the hospital and home with me. I know that was nothing but the Lord working on my behalf. You see what God will do if you serve Him? That was just the start of good things to come.

As the world welcomed JFK and his new regime in 1961, my wife and I welcomed our daughter, Cassandra into the world. Our family had grown larger and I started praying about ways to better take care of them. While my wife was receiving compensation out on maternity leave, we still needed to supplement our income. The Lord was prodding me to do more. I began to set my sights on opening my own business.

Blacks elsewhere were having new experiences; some of them good, some of them bad. In 1962, James Howard Meredith, after being denied admission three times, was finally admitted into the University of Mississippi (Ole Miss). Ross Barnett, the governor of Louisiana at the time, blocked Meredith's admission. Only after being forced, the United States Federal

Marshals escorted him to class until he graduated in August of 1963 due to racial tension on campus.

In sports, Jackie Robinson was inducted into the Cooperstown, NY Baseball Hall of Fame on July 3, 1962 and the first Heisman Trophy was awarded to an African American. It was given to Ernie Davis, the running back from Syracuse. Sadly, that same year he was diagnosed with leukemia and passed away.

A military accomplishment, Samuel L. Gravely was appointed captain of the Navy Destroyer Escort, *U.S.S. Falgout.* He became the first African American to command a United States warship. He later received the rank of Rear Admiral, also a first for African Americans.

The year 1963 is remembered by so many for a variety of different reasons. For those who followed his career, there was much to be celebrated because Sidney Poitier became the first African American to win an Academy Award for his role in *Lillies of the Field.* That was one good thing that happened in 1963. But, as is always the case in life, there were many not so good things that happened in that year.

While President John F. Kennedy was petitioning Congress to strengthen voting rights, create more jobs and enforce school integration across the nation, the Sixteenth Street Baptist Church in Birmingham, AL became the site of a vicious attack. On September 15, 1963 four little girls were killed as a bomb was thrown into the church where they were seated during Sunday School.

The murder of the four little girls was especially devastating because it took place on the heels of what is now called the, "March on Washington." Baynard Rustin and A. Phillip Randolph organized the march where over 250,000 protestors marched to bring attention to the crisis in America concerning housing, jobs and education. Having taken place on August 23, 1963, it was this noteworthy day that Dr. Martin Luther King Jr. delivered his most famous speech,

"I Have a Dream" at the foot of the Lincoln Memorial.

Some may remember 1963 as the year that Dr. King, Dr. Ralph Abernathy and Reverend Fred L. Shuttlesworth led a series of marches in Birmingham, AL to protest the severe racial injustices aimed at African Americans. Over 1,500 protestors were arrested in the marches that often resulted in violence. One such arrestee was Dr. King himself. Attack dogs and fire hoses were often used on the protestors, even women and children. The violence that ensued from such events caused outrage amongst many White Americans who joined the protest for civil rights in America for African Americans. Police Chief, "Bull" Connor, and Governor, George Wallace became the poster-children for American racism and segregation. While incarcerated during one of these protests, and thinking about all of the injustice and racial inequality that he and our people faced at that time, Dr. King was inspired to write the famous, "Letter from a Birmingham Jail."

The protests were not the only place where the bully, George Wallace, showed his face. He was a very visible force in the efforts not to allow students, Vivian Malone and James Hood, to enter the University of Alabama. They had to be ushered around by the National Guard as people like Governor Wallace and others tried to physically keep them from entering the University.

Sadly, some may remember 1963 as the year we lost two of America's heroes; John F. Kennedy and Medgar Evers. In the office of President at the time, John Kennedy was assassinated in a moving motorcade in Dallas, TX. Mr. Evers, a Civil Rights leader and field secretary for the NAACP, was assassinated in front of his home in Jackson, MS.

While it seemed that there was turmoil on every hand, the Lord was still on the throne. I, too, have memories of 1963. It was the year that changed my life forever.

I was still working on the job that my sister had gotten me as an attendant at a gas station. I was diligently working one day and the owner came in and wanted to talk to me. We went to the office to talk and he told me that he had to let me go because the payroll was too high. In essence, he was overextended and he needed to downsize. So, since I was the last one hired, I was the first one fired. It could not have happened at a worse time. My wife and I were trying to buy a home. We had a young family and she was freshly out on maternity leave. I knew the Lord was testing me. I went home and told my wife what had happened. I told her not to worry because I knew that the Lord was going to take care of us.

I picked up the Washington Post. I saw that there was an opening in a shop at 4400 Wisconsin Avenue. The guy that owned the shop needed an automobile mechanic. I saw the ad on

Thursday and went to see him on Friday. He had me to fill out an application and asked me when I wanted to start work. I told him that if hired, I wanted to start on Monday. He then told me that he had some work over the weekend and asked me to start the very next day. I told him that I could not work on Sundays because Sunday is the Lords' day. So, I put my tool box in my little car and went to work on Saturday. God was just blessing me!

We discussed my pay and he asked if I'd like to work on consignment. I wasn't exactly sure what consignment was because I'd been used to working for a set amount. But in essence, working on consignment was just getting a certain percentage of parts and labor. I received ten percent of the price of all the labor that I performed on top of my regular salary. I was making out pretty good. I was making about $200 a week or a little better. If I did a good job, sometimes I would have an extra $40-50 in tips before the week was out.

I worked there and was happy to do it, but the Lord impressed upon me to open up my own shop–my own business. We were paying someone to babysit the children when my wife went back to work. She was making a salary and we were comfortable taking care of our expenses, but the Lord was telling me that there was yet more. I sat down and talked to my wife about what the Lord had placed in my heart. I asked her for her trust and help with venturing out and doing what the Lord had instructed me to do. She did. *She openeth her mouth with wisdom; and in her tongue is the law of kindness." Proverbs 31:26.*

My wife and I put our capital together to start the new business. The first part of it I used to put in an application for a Shell Station on Georgia Avenue and Park Road. (I got it!!) We put the remainder of the money into the station and started our business.

By the end of 1963, I had accumulated so much business I didn't have room to contain it. It was time to expand.

While I was expanding my business, the United States was expanding too. There were three noteworthy accomplishments in the area of Civil Rights, and more specifically for Dr. Martin Luther King Jr. *Time* magazine did a feature article and proclaimed him "Man of the Year." He was present as President Lyndon Johnson signed into ratification the bill that passed the Civil Rights Act of 1964. It made provisions for the elimination of discrimination in education, employment and public accommodations. And he received the Nobel Peace Prize in Oslo, Norway.

In arts and entertainment, the Supremes with Diana Ross, were topping the charts with songs like "Baby Love" and "Where Did Our Love Go?"

Fannie Lou Hamer, an American voting rights activist and civil rights leader, single-handedly brought worldwide attention to the fact that Blacks were refused delegate representation by the Democratic Party. She assisted in forming and was the Vice-President of the Mississippi

Freedom Democratic Party. Their work led to the inclusion of representation by African Americans by the next convention in 1968.

Also a civil rights accomplishment, the 24th amendment was ratified. Its ratification outlawed poll taxes that kept African Americans, most in the southern states, from voting. Poll taxes varied depending on the state the voter lived in, but in most cases, the tax was between $1 and $2. This was a huge burden to African Americans, as the tax was imposed upon them when the annual salary was less than $5,000. Sometimes African Americans were even asked to pay this tax several times prior to be allowed to vote. This was burdensome and prevented a lot of African Americans from voting.

I mentioned earlier that the business on Georgia Avenue had grown so large that I needed to expand. Let me explain how God's favor was continually working. I was looking at a place on Dean Avenue. I needed a little extra cash, so I went to the Small Business Association (SBA) to ask for a certain amount, but the Lord had gone before me and He had another plan. I put in an application for $3,000. When the officer called me to talk about the loan, they asked if I was going to keep both stations open. I said, "Yes!" The Loan Officer told me that since I'd done so well on Georgia Avenue, that they would increase my loan amount from $3,000 to $5,000. I said, "Thank you, God!"

On December 7, 1964, I opened shop on Dean Avenue. The loan officer projected that I would probably sell about 35,000 gallons per year in that location. I sold 47,000 gallons in that month alone! The total gallons sold only fell below that amount twice. From there, we were selling between 60-70,000 gallons a month on a regular basis. I didn't get big-headed though. I knew that it was nothing that I did, but only the hand of God. He was blessing me. My wife was able to stay home for 16 years to raise our children. It wasn't until the children were getting out of school that she decided to go back to work.

In 1965 I met a man from NY who came to meet me and talk about my life. He'd heard about my success with the gas stations. In a time when many Blacks weren't able to even get loans or start businesses, I was not only doing it, but doing it well. He was in publishing and wanted to encourage me to write a book about being a Black man in business to help other Blacks who wanted to start their own businesses. I loved to help people, and I believe that was just the Lord sowing the seeds for the book that you are holding in your hands today.

So, 1965 was like the year of big dreams for me, especially with the business doing so well. It was also a big year for Civil Rights, Black society and government.

In government, Thurgood Marshall was appointed to the position of Solicitor General of the United States by President Lyndon Johnson. That was a pretty big deal. The Solicitor General is responsible for conducting all litigation on behalf of the United States in the Supreme Court, and to supervise the handling of litigation in the federal appellate courts.

Patricia Harris became the first African American woman appointed an ambassador. She served in the country of Luxembourg as appointed by President Lyndon Johnson. Under the presidency of Jimmy Carter, she was the first African American woman appointed to a cabinet position.

In March of 1965, Dr. King led the famous march from Selma to Montgomery, Alabama. When marchers crossed the Edmund Petus Bridge, they were met with extreme violence. Local police met them and used billy clubs, tear gas, and cattle prods to beat the marchers, showing their resistance to voter rights and the freedom to petition for those rights. That day has sadly been coined "Bloody Sunday." The date was March 25, 1965.

In that same vein, federal troops were called in to curtail the violence as America experienced one of its most violent and destructive race riots in Watts, CA. The Watts Riots of 1965 refers to a large-scale racial war which lasted 6 days in the Watts neighborhood of Los Angeles, California, in August 1965. By the time the riot subsided, 34 people had been killed, 1,032 injured, and 3,952 arrested. Property losses were upwards of $225 million. It would stand as the worst riot in Los Angeles history until eclipsed by the Los Angeles riots of 1992.

It seems that 1965 was a bloody year. Both Malcolm X, and white civil rights worker, Viola Gregg Liuzzo were assassinated. Malcolm X was killed while he was giving a speech in the Audubon Ballroom in NYC, and Mrs. Liuzzo was gunned down as she drove some black members from Selma after Martin Luther King's march. Her only crime was not having hatred in her heart for other races.

One good thing that happened, though, was that President Johnson signed the 1965 Voting Rights Act into law to give all people the right to vote regardless of creed or color.

Previous revisions did not include equality for voting for all people, revisions were made as often as possible to afford each race the same rights.

African Americans in government had a lot to celebrate in 1966. Dr. Robert Weaver became the first African American to serve in the President of the United States' Cabinet. He was Secretary of Housing and Urban Development under President Lyndon B. Johnson. The United States Department of Housing and Urban Development, also known as HUD, is a Cabinet department in the Executive branch of the federal government. Although its beginnings were in the House and Home Financing Agency, it was founded as a Cabinet department in 1965, as part of the "Great Society" program of President Lyndon B. Johnson, to develop and execute policy on housing and cities, and urban housing matters.

Also under President Lyndon Johnson, Andrew Felton Brimmer became the first African

American appointed to serve on the prestigious Federal Reserve Board. The Federal Reserve Board determines how everyone in America lends money by coordinating the banks and defining the value of the dollar. A Governor on the board maintains contact with each of the 12 region's bank presidents, economic analysts, and their regional directors.

Edward W. Brooke, a Republican attorney general from Massachusetts, was elected to a Senate seat in Congress. There had not been an African American elected to serve in the U.S. Senate since the Reconstruction Period.

A breakthrough for women, 1966 saw two African American women elected to state political offices. Yvonne Brathwaite Burke was elected to the California assembly and Barbara Jordan was elected to the Texas State Senate. Both Burke and Jordan were elected to the U.S. House of Representatives in 1972.

Constance Baker Motley, the former president of the borough of Manhattan, made history by becoming the first African American federal judge as appointed by President Johnson. Years later she would move up to become the Senior District Court Judge covering several New York counties.

The Black Panthers, a black self-defense group aimed at getting revolutionary changes made in America's policies as they related to oppressed African Americans, was organized in Oakland, CA by Bobby Seale and Huey P. Newton. Eldridge Cleaver and Fred Hampton were also members of the organization.

Stokely Carmichael, the head of the Student Nonviolent Coordinating Committee, introduced the slogan, "Black Power," in the liberation struggles of voter registration in Mississippi.

In the field of Science, Dr. Samuel M. Nabrit became the first African American to serve as a member of the Atomic Energy Commission. Dr. Nabrit was president of Texas Southern College/University (HBCU), from 1955-1966.

His brother, James Nabrit, was president of Howard University from 1960-1969, also an HBCU.

Julian Bond won an elected seat in the State of Georgia House of Representatives. However, he was refused his seat due to his open views opposing American involvement in the Vietnam War. After a bitter court battle, Bond was seated but treated as a pariah by his colleagues.

In arts and entertainment, Leontyne Price opened the new season at the New York Met in an opera written exclusively for her, Samuel Barber's, *Anthony and Cleopatra.*

It was clear that Lyndon B. Johnson's administration was serious about making changes in the way that America operated. He believed in putting the best people in place to get things done no matter what color their skin was. That, and God's extreme favor on his life, enabled Thurgood Marshall to be appointed to the United States Supreme Court. He was the first African

American to ever be appointed to the high court as an Associate Justice.

While Chief Justice Marshall was making strides inside the highest court in the land, there was utter lawlessness happening outside. The summer of 1967 was called the "Hot Summer." There were over forty race riots in major metropolitan areas throughout the U.S. In an effort to investigate these matters, President Johnson appointed a National Advisory Commission on Civil Disorders that became known as Kerner Commission.

In an effort to put an end to the violence at home and abroad, Dr. King denounced the United States' involvement in the Vietnam War on March 24, 1967. His unpopular stance said that "Blacks and Whites should seek to resist this war by becoming *conscientious objectors*."

In science, Major Robert H. Lawrence Jr. became the first African American astronaut on June 30, 1967. He was a research scientist and pilot. Unfortunately, he was killed when his jet crashed in the California desert.

My faith was radically changed and challenged in 1968. I've always considered my faith to be strong. I met the Lord at a very young age and made it my business to try to stay in His word and to put all of my trust in Him. It's a good thing that I started early because that year, for sure, I needed it.

The "Hot Summer" changed my business. The riots really affected the bottom line profits of the operation. I had two businesses but I couldn't be in two places at one time so I enlisted some help. This is when things took a really bad turn. I was trying to be a Christian and help my fellow brother the way that the Lord had helped me. I had been trying to find a good manager. I tried training up the guys that said they wanted to go into business for themselves but it wasn't quite working out. I had to fire the first guy that I hired as a manager. The second one stayed around for awhile and when things got too hectic, I turned the Dean Avenue location over to him. Sadly, less than two years later, he was out of business. This is one of the downfalls of having your own business. You can never really know who to trust. I got burned more than once.

I was changing and so was America. "Afro American" and "Black" were the new names by which Black people wanted to be called. "Negro" was out.

Shirley Chisholm became the first African American woman elected to Congress. Four years later she made a bid for the Presidency of the United States, becoming the first black woman to take on this challenge. She entered the primaries in twelve states.

The Civil Rights Bill of 1968 was signed into law. It included the Fair Housing Act that prohibited discrimination on the basis of race in the renting and sale of apartments and houses.

Howard University was the target for demonstrations by students demanding a curriculum that was more inclusive of black culture. It was out of these protests that Black Studies programs came to the forefront.

There were two great losses for the American people in 1968. One of them was the brother of the late President John F. Kennedy, Senator Robert F. Kennedy. He was assassinated while addressing well wishers on his victory in the California Democratic primary. The other, an especially hard loss for me, was the loss of Dr. Martin Luther King, Jr. He was shot and killed on April 4, 1968 while standing on a balcony at the Lorraine Motel, in Memphis, TN. Ralph D. Abernathy succeeded Dr. King as the head of the SCLC. The very next month, in the true spirit of Dr. King, he led a march on Washington called the "Poor People's March."

In 1969, African Americans felt like some justice had been served when James Earl Ray pled guilty to the assassination of Dr. King and was sentenced to ninety-nine years in prison. Even though a man was losing his life, we felt some justice for having lost one of our heroes.

As a result of student sit-ins and the protests lodged from Howard University, Harvard University established its first Afro American Studies program. It set the stage for similar programs around the country.

In arts and entertainment, there was more celebrating to be done, as James Earl Jones won a Tony Award for his role as Jack Johnson in *The Great White Hope* on Broadway.

Moneta Sleet, Jr. became the first African American to win a Pulitzer Prize for Photography.

Arthur Mitchell, the first African American to dance as a principal performer with the American Ballet Company in 1955, established his dance company, "The Dance Theater of Harlem."

6

1970-1979

No one would ever dispute that the 1960's were a turbulent time in America and the chaotic events seemed destined to continue into the 1970's. The major trends that defined this decade included a growing disillusionment of government, advances in civil rights, increased influence of the women's movement, a heightened concern for the environment, and increased space exploration. Many of the "radical" ideas of the 60's gained wider acceptance in the new decade, and were mainstreamed into American life and culture. Amid war, social realignment and presidential impeachment proceedings, American culture flourished. The events of the times were reflected in, and became the inspiration for, much of the music, literature, entertainment, and even fashion of the decade.

The population was about 204,879,000. Of those, 4,088,000 were unemployed. The National debt was $382 billion and the average salary was $7,564. Milk was around $.33 a quart, bread was $.24 a loaf and round steaks were $1.30 a pound. The life expectancy of males and females, respectively, were 67.1 and 74.8.

During the seventies the Lord continued to bless my family. In 1970, the average income for Blacks was $22,000 and I was making a salary that was significantly higher than that. That is not said to brag on my own abilities, for without Christ I am nothing. *"I can do all things through Christ which strengtheneth me."* Philippians 4:13. I said that to encourage you to give thanks and praise to God and acknowledge Him for all of His works in your life. The Lord blessed me because He knew that I would be careful to give Him all of the credit for my success. With the help of the Lord, I had a good measure of success during those years, but I wasn't the only one that the Lord had His hand on.

Dr. Clifton R. Wharton, Jr. crossed over a huge hurdle when he became the first African American selected to preside over a large university. In January of 1970, he became the president of Michigan State University in Lansing, Michigan. To me, this was a major feat because the school systems weren't even fully integrated.

Essence magazine, which is still very much alive today, issued its first publication. Its dedication to showing the positive views and stories of African Americans were appreciated and necessary because of the crude way that Blacks had been portrayed by the media.

I attend a mid-day Bible Study at my church on Wednesdays. There was a lady there, Louise, who was so funny. I used to tell her all of the time that she reminded me of the Flip Wilson character, *Geraldine,* who got his start in 1970. He had a prime-time variety show called *The Flip*

Wilson Show. I watched it as much as I could. He was only the second African American to host such a show, after Nat King Cole in the fifties.

While Flip Wilson was tickling our funny bone with his *Geraldine* and *Reverend Leroy* characters, Toni Morrison was tugging on our heartstrings with her first published book, *The Bluest Eye.*

Jimi Hendrix, one of the main figures responsible for producing new musical sounds by infusing jazz and heavy metal, died in London, England of a suspected drug overdose.

The America that we know today, with its opportunities for advancement and a more inclusive assortment of people who can lay hold to the "American Dream," is so, in part, because of the changes that the people demanded and fought for in the 1970's.

In 1971, in an effort to employ a tool that could speed up the integration of public schools, the United States Supreme court ruled in favor of busing. Desegregation busing, also known as busing, is the practice of attempting to integrate schools by assigning students to schools based primarily on race, rather than geographic proximity.

An organization whose only agenda was economic and political action called, *PUSH* (People United to Save Humanity), was organized and led by the Reverend Jesse Jackson. Stemming from the Black Panther Party organized a few years prior, there was a movement initiated called the "Black Power Movement." It was one of the most significant movements in regards to its social, political and cultural aspects. The movement received a lot of heat because of "radical" ideas and style. It had provocative rhetoric; its followers' militant posture altered the contours of American identity. They were deeply involved and entrenched in the local communities. For this reason, they were accused of subversive activity and closely monitored. J. Edgar Hoover, the director of the FBI at the time, worked hard to expose and find charges to label the group as "extremists that need to be watched." On his list of people that should be watched were: Angela Davis, African American scholar, political activist, and UCLA professor; Eldridge Cleaver, author and prominent figure in the Black Panther Party; Bobby Seale, civil rights activist and revolutionary and co-founder of the Black Panther Party; and Huey P. Newton who founded the Afro American society and co-founded the Black Panther Party. Many others had been killed in police raids in 1969.

With all of the political turmoil and fights that were taking place in America, there was some reprieve to be had at the movies. The number one movie of that time was a movie that I saw and loved, *Shaft*. It was directed by Gordon Parks and the song, "Shaft" won an Academy Award as Best Song.

In Sports, Leroy "Satchel" Paige became the first African American pitcher elected to the Baseball Hall of Fame.

While Satchel was throwing sliders and fastballs, I was throwing some things together myself. I was approached by a realtor who was looking for people to invest in land in Westmoreland County, VA on Stratford Harbor. There were about five miles of beach area that had been staked out on the Potomac River. I was, and still am, always looking to be a part of a wealth-creating business. I always wanted to have something in place, financially, so that my wife and children would be secure if something should happen to me. With that in mind, I secured three lots on the waterfront.

The area was beautiful. There were clubhouses, swimming pools, tennis and basketball courts there for the enjoyment of the residents. We would take the kids there in the summers. My thinking was that the income from the land would finance my children's college tuition. As time went on I sold all of the lots.

A survey in 1972 revealed that forty-two percent of all prison inmates were African

Americans. That was one of the facts taken into consideration when the US Supreme Court ruled, on June 29th, that the death penalty was unconstitutional. More than half of the six hundred prisoners held on Death Row were African American.

On the other end of the spectrum, there were some black men that were doing extraordinary things. James M. Rodgers, Jr. from Durham, NC was one such man. He became the first African American named National Teacher of the Year.

Andrew Young was another man doing positive things in society. He, along with Barbara Jordan of Texas, and Yvonne Brathwaite Burke of California, were all elected to the U.S. House of Representatives.

There were two great scandals unveiled in 1972. A black security guard's discovery of a break-in at the headquarters of the Democratic National Committee's office was the catalyst for the investigation of the Watergate Scandal. The

Tuskegee Syphilis Study was also revealed in 1972. Remember that the synopsis of the Tuskegee Study is that 300 African American males from impoverished, Macon County, Alabama, were given syphilis and left untreated in an experiment to see what would happen to humans if the disease wasn't treated. For 40 years, this study and its findings were kept from the general public by the US Public Health Service Dept. But the Lord has a way of bringing light to all darkness. *"And art confident that thou thyself art a guide of the blind, a light of them which are in darkness."* Romans 2:19

In 1973, a young lady, Marion Wright Edeman, who like myself, had a passion for ministering to poor people, established the Children's Defense Fund. It was an organization designed to advocate for the rights of minorities, the poor and disabled.

Another wonderful event that first began in 1973 was the recognition of Dr. Martin Luther

King Jr. with a state holiday. Illinois was the first state to pass this legislation.

Those were two highlights of great events/organizations that began in 1973. But there was more praise to be given to God because of something that ended. The Vietnam War officially ended on March 29, 1973.

There were plenty of historical firsts in 1974. In government, Tennessee sent its first African American representative, Harold Ford, to Congress.

Jill Brown made history in aviation by becoming the first African American, female pilot in the Armed Forces. Four years later, in 1978, she became the first African American female pilot to fly for a major airline.

There were two major first in sports as well. Henry "Hank" Aaron hit his 715th home run, in 1974, breaking Babe Ruth's long-standing record of 714. Frank Robinson became the first African American manager for the Cleveland Indians.

Beverly Johnson became the first African American to be featured on the cover of Vogue magazine.

Richard Nixon became the first president to resign from office. His decision was based on the Watergate scandal and the possibility of an impeachment trial. I was very interested in the events surrounding the Watergate scandal. I tried to watch the trial and all surrounding events whenever I could.

Closing out 1974, we said goodbye to Duke Ellington. He was the father of many musical firsts.

When 1975 came in, Blacks were still pushing to create a deeper, more permanent mark in this land we call the United States.

Making his mark in tennis, Arthur Ashe, paving the way for the young Williams' sisters, became the first African American to win the men's singles at Wimbledon. He defeated Jimmy Connors, the final score 1-6.

Credited with setting up their own independently owned television station, Dr. William V. Banks and his associates opened WGDR in Detroit, Michigan in 1975. It was on a television station much like this one that one of my favorite television shows, *The Jeffersons*, first aired. It ran for eleven seasons.

Celebrating another victory in military achievement, General Daniel "Chappie" James, Jr. became the first African American Four Star General in the United States Air Force on August 29, 1975. And the military achievements continue in 1976 when Janie L. Mines became the first African American female cadet to enter the U.S. Naval Academy. This was the first year that the academy admitted women of any race.

Pinning another feather in the fight for race and gender equality, it was in 1976 that Barbara Jordan delivered an address as the keynote speaker at the Democratic National Convention. Her address stirred the nation.

Another female cutting her own path in 1976 was Patricia Robert Harris. She became the first African American woman appointed to a cabinet position when Jimmy Carter appointed her Secretary of Housing and Urban development.

The death penalty was reinstated by the Supreme Court in 1976. It was felt by the affirmative justices, and I agree, that the death penalty aids in the determent of major crimes.

But, to end the achievements and significance of this year on a more positive note, there were statistics that showed a sharp rise in college and university enrollment for African American students from 282,000 in 1966 to 1,062,000 in 1976.

In 1977, justice was finally served when Robert E. Chambliss, a former Ku Klux Klan member, was found guilty for the deaths of the four teenage girls killed in the Montgomery, Alabama church bombing fourteen years earlier.

In civil rights, Karen Farmer broke the racial barrier of the Daughters of the American

Revolution (DAR) by becoming the first African American accepted into membership. Her acceptance was based on her kinship to American Revolutionary War veteran, William Hood.

Continuing in his legacy of trying to right the racial wrongs of previous years, President Jimmy Carter post humously awarded the Medal of Freedom to Dr. Martin Luther King, Jr. President Carter also named another African American, Clifford Alexander, Jr., Secretary of the Army.

There were three young men in 1978 who were very surprised that despite the racial barriers that existed in the U.S., their dreams of becoming astronauts came true. They were Frederick Gregory, Ronald E. McNair and Guion S. Bluford.

Faye Wattleton became the President of Planned Parenthood Federation of America.

In 1978, Morehouse School of Medicine opened its doors.

Closing out the events that celebrate significant achievements for African Americans in the 1970's, 1979 yielded big results in the way of accomplishments in the armed forces. Frank Peterson Jr. became the 1st African American to earn the rank of General in the U.S. Marines. Hazel Johnson became the first African American woman to be promoted to the rank of General in the US Army.

While the U.S. Civil Rights Commission disclosed that 46% of African American students were still attending all-Black schools, despite the ruling of the Supreme Court to integrate, the Lord raised up Richard Arrington, Jr. to become the first African American mayor of Birmingham, AL. Birmingham, at that time, was considered to be one of the most racist cities in America. But that's how the Lord works. When the enemy thinks that he has you in one area, the Lord is raising up help in another.

In that same year, God blessed Arthur Lewis and allowed him to win the Nobel Prize in economics. He is a Jamaican born American and professor of Economics at Princeton University in New Jersey.

Breaking ground in the area of philanthropy, Franklin D. Thomas became the first African American to head a major philanthropic foundation-the Ford Foundation. The Ford Foundation is a private foundation created to fund programs that focus on strengthening democratic values, community and economic development, education, media, arts and culture, and human rights

The 1970's were good years for African Americans and for me. I'm grateful to God to be able to say that my businesses did really well during those times. In fact, the Lord showed us so much favor, and we did so much business, that we were able to pay off all of our debts. It's a wonderful thing to be able to say that you don't owe anyone anything. The Lord allowed that to be my testimony. The doctors and the hospitals that I owed for treating Valerie were paid in full.

All bill collectors were paid in full. That's how the Lord wants us to live. He gave his life so that we could live more abundantly. So when He blesses us, we should be responsible with what He gives us. We should pay our tithes and offering. At the end of the day the only person that we should owe is God for what He's done for us. *"For the Lord is great and greatly to be praised: He is to be feared above all gods" Psalms 96:4.*

7

1980-1989

The population in 1980 was 227,250,000. Twelve percent, or about 26,500,000 were African American and eighty-five percent of them populated urban central cites. The national debt was $914 billion. The average salary was $15,575 and minimum wage was $3.10. The life expectancy of males and females were 69.9 and 77.6 respectively.

The United States celebrated its 200th birthday during this decade and billionaires like Leona Helmsley and Ivan Boesky, were amongst the many that got caught up in the spirit of splurge that seemed to surround the 1980's.

President Reagan was in office and declared a war on drugs. We, as African Americans, lost many of our finest talents to a growing disease called AIDS, which, by the end of the 1980's had spread significantly to Black and Hispanic women. To make matters worse, unemployment was on the rise. Yet, in spite of it all, we were still striving and thriving.

Of the twelve percent of African Americans in the population, there was one man, in particular, who stood out in the field of science. His name was Dr. Levi Watkins, Jr. and he was the first doctor to place an automatic defibrillator in the human heart to help blood flow properly.

In the field of aviation, Naval aviator, Charles Frank Bolden, Jr. was selected by NASA as a US astronaut.

In sports, the 1980 Winter Olympics made way for the first Blacks ever to compete at the games. Robert Hickey, Jeff Jordan, Willie Davenport, the oldest member of the team at 36, Jeffrey Gadley, Howard Siler, Jr., Joseph Tyler, Jeff Jost, and Dick Nalley were participants of the 1980 bobsleigh event.

As we were celebrating taking more steps forward, the revelation that the KKK had set up a training camp for new recruits in Cullman, AL seemed to knock us back a few. But our spirits were too strong. The more they pushed us, the more we pushed ourselves.

A young man named Robert Johnson pushed in the world of television and began operating Black Entertainment Television (BET) out of Washington, DC. Eleven years later, he was still pushing as BET became the first completely African American owned company to be treated on the New York Stock Exchange.

When 1981 rolled in, we were still pushing. On the literary scene, Pamela McAllister Johnson became the first African American woman to publish a widely circulated newspaper, the Ithaca Journal.

In Arts & Entertainment, Jennifer Holiday and Lena Horne took center stage at the Tony Awards. Jennifer Holiday for being the major star in the Broadway hit musical, *Dreamgirls,* and Ms.

Horne for her hit one-woman show, *Lena Horne: The Lady and Her Music.*

In October of 1981, the wife of the late Dr. Martin Luther King Jr. opened the MLK Library and Archives. She established this facility for one of the same reasons that I am writing this book. She didn't want his memory, his many written speeches and the accounts of his life, to be forgotten.

And, in the spirit of MLK, Labor Unions and Civil Rights organizations marched on Washington, DC to protest Ronald Reagan's policy toward organized labor, cuts in social programs, and changes in job security. This was called "Solidarity Day" and over 260,000,000 marchers were in attendance.

The year 1982 was successful for African Americans in various areas.

In Arts & Entertainment, two men caught the attention of the whole world. The first was Mr. Bryant Gumbel. He was the first African American to anchor a national news program at

NBC television. The second was Simon Lamont Estes. After making a tour in the world's finest Opera houses, he made his debut at the MET in New York City in *Tannhauser.*

There were two Pulitzer Prize winning pieces of literature that came out in 1982. The first was Alice Walker's, *The Color Purple.* Three years later the book became the movie, *The Color Purple.* The second was Charles Fuller's play, *A Soldier's Play.* It was done with the "Negro Ensemble" and later the screenplay, like *The Color Purple,* was developed from it, for the movie *A Soldier's Story.*

In sports, Henry "Hank" Aaron, the home run king of the National League, was elected to the Baseball Hall of Fame.

Continuing the forward momentum in the political arena, African Americans, in 1983, were mayors in many of the largest cities in the United States.

President Reagan signed a bill into law that made the third Monday in January a holiday honoring the life of Dr. Martin Luther King, Jr. In this same year, President Reagan extended the Voting Rights Act of 1965 by signing the bill into law.

Katie Beatrice Hall, Edolphus Towns, and Alan Wheat were all elected to Congress.

In science, Colonel Guion S. Bluford Jr. became the first African American to actually fly in space. He was chosen to be a part of the Space Shuttle Mission that flew the shuttle, *Challenger*.

Soaring high above the clouds in the area of Arts & Entertainment was singer and songwriter, Michael Jackson. His song, *Thriller*, became the biggest selling record in US History. It won eight Grammy Awards and sold over thirty million copies around the world.

While Michael Jackson was being crowned the King of Pop, Vanessa Williams was being crowned the first African American woman to win the title of Miss America. I'm not sure if it was a set up or not, but she was later made to give the crown back as some photos of her in an adult magazine were uncovered.

The year 1984 allowed Blacks to make significant power moves in the area of government/law. Jesse Jackson became a hero when he was able to get the release of the US Navy pilot , Robert Goodman. His plane was shot down and he was being held captive.

Robert Nix Jr., who became the first African American to serve on a State Supreme Court in Pennsylvania, became Chief Justice of that same court.

Thirty-one African American mayors were elected or reelected in 1984.

Becoming the highest ranking woman of color in the armed forces, in 1985 Sherian Grace Cadoria was promoted to Brigadier General in the US Army.

In Arts & Entertainment, television brought the case of the Black radical group, *The Move*, into the world's forefront. They were bombed out by the state police, killing eleven members and destroying two Philadelphia city blocks. Eleven years later, in 1996, a federal jury found the city and two former top officials liable for the deadly incident. The Lord gets vengeance in His own time.

Quincy Jones' produced, "We Are the World" single, written by both Michael Jackson and Lionel Ritchie, could be heard on radio stations around the world. Many voices, to include Tina Turner, Dionne Warwick, Stevie Wonder, Billy Joel, Diana Ross, Kenny Rogers and Willie Nelson sang on the release. It was a song that won almost as many awards as it had voices singing on it. The proceeds from the famed song went to aid and famine relief in Africa.

The famed Apollo Theater reopened its doors after a $10M renovation.

As changes at the Apollo in the North were taking place, there was some moving and shaking going on in the South as well, especially in the Lieutenant Governor's office. In 1986, Lawrence Douglas Wilder was elected as the

Lieutenant Governor of Virginia. Four years later he was sworn in as the first African American elected as a state Governor in VA.

The year 1986 marked the first time that the birthday of Dr. Martin Luther King Jr.'s birthday was celebrated as a federal holiday.

In sports, Mike Tyson was making headlines by becoming the youngest boxer to become the World Boxing Council Heavyweight Champion of the world.

It was in 1986 that we lost a great scientist that we'd only 8 years prior celebrated. Ronald E. McNair was killed aboard the space shuttle, *Challenger*. But his death was but a seed. That seed flourished in Dr. Mae Carol Jamison who in 1987 became the first African American woman astronaut chosen to train at NASA in the US Space Program.

The Office of Brigadier General had a big year in 1987. Bernard P. Randolph was promoted to the rank of Brigadier General in the US Air Force and Fred A. Gorden, who already held the office, was appointed Commandant of the Cadets at West Point Military Academy.

There was a major accomplishment in the world of science in that year. An African American pediatric neurosurgeon named Ben Carson, led a team in the separation of Siamese twins connected at the head. To go from not being recognized as a human during slavery times, to heading this incredible surgery, that is nothing but the Lord's favor and grace on our people.

Another man that the Lord raised up to be watched was Clifton R. Wharton. He became the first Black Chairman and CEO of a major US corporation by heading TIAA-CREF, the Teachers Insurance and Annuity Association-College Retirement Equities Fund. It was then the 19th largest Fortune 500 Company with assets of $290 billion. He served until 1993 when he became Deputy Secretary under President Clinton.

And in sports, Earvin "Magic" Johnson, sprinkled a little magic on the courts as he led his team to five championships and won the NBA's MVP award in 1988.

Continuing our celebration of achievements of Blacks in sports, Florence "Flo Jo" Griffith Joyner and quarterback for the Redskins, Doug Williams, had great years. Mrs. Joyner at the 1988 Olympics won three gold and one silver medals and Doug Williams was named MVP in Super Bowl XXII.

Debbie Thomas became the first African American to win a medal at the Winter Olympics. She won a bronze medal in figure skating.

Jesse Jackson made a bid for the Presidency of the United States in 1988. He lost the democratic nomination to Michael Dukakis, but helped to secure 1200 delegates to the Democratic camp.

Spelman College had a lot to celebrate that year. William "Bill" Cosby donated twenty million dollars to the college, becoming the first African American to ever present that large a gift.

In Arts and entertainment, Blacks were beginning to ascend into their places as stars in front of *and* behind the big screen, as director, Spike Lee's "School Daze" and "Coming to America" starring Eddie Murphy came out. They were both huge box office hits.

The fall of 1988 was a trying year for me. In August, I underwent subdural hematoma surgery at Georgetown Hospital in Washington, DC. I had three operations on my head. I was hospitalized for the entire month of August. At one point the doctors called my family in because they thought that I would not make it. My family went into prayer and called on the name of the Lord. God worked a miracle in my life. He healed my body and gave me back my sight.

After lying on my back for 30 days, my bones had frozen. The doctors thought, at first, that another operation was going to be needed to break and reset the bones. However, a second opinion suggested that intense physical therapy and exercise would be able to correct the problems. I had to learn how to walk all over again. Through many sessions of physical therapy, and God's healing touch, I am healed. I truly thank God.

I promised God if He healed my body that I would testify to His goodness every time I had a chance. This is why I continue to give God the praise!

I had a lot to celebrate that year. With all of its ups and downs, huge gains and losses, I finally retired from the oil business in 1988. At the age of 63, I hung my hat and walked away with my 5, 10, 15, and 20 year plaques from Shell Oil company. We had a good run but the time had come for us to close our doors.

Closing out the 1980's, 1989 was a very successful year for African Americans in government. It was, again, a year with many firsts. William Gray III was selected as the first African American House Majority Whip. David Denkins, beating out District Attorney Rudolph Giuliani, became the first African American mayor of New York City. Ronald H. Brown was elected Chairperson of the Democratic National

Convention. It was, and still is, one of the most powerful political positions on the Democratic party. Colin Powell, at age 52, became the youngest and the first African American military person to be named Chairman of the Joint Chiefs of Staff, the highest office in the nation's military. The only African American to ever serve in President George Bush's cabinet, Dr. Louis W. Sullivan, president of Morehouse College of Medicine, was selected to serve as the Secretary of Health and Human Services.

In education, Temple University in Philadelphia, PA became the first university in the United States to offer a Doctoral degree in African American studies.

And finally, businessman Kenneth I. Chenault, was elected to the position of president of the Consumer Card and Financial Services Division of American Express.

8   1990-1999

The 1990s were truly the electronic age. Though I am not yet internet savvy, the World Wide Web was born in 1992, changing the way we communicate (email), spend our money (online gambling, stores), and do business (e-commerce). By 1994, 3 million people were online. And by 1998, this figure increased to 100 million people. It was estimated that by 2001, some 1 billion people will be connected.

In 1990, America was involved in another war. In a battle called "Operation Desert Storm," President George H. W. Bush, committed over 500,000 American troops to convince Saddam Hussein to withdraw from Kuwait.

While we waited on our knees in prayer for our young men and women to come home from overseas in that battle, we celebrated as Nelson Mandela was released after twenty-seven years in prison. Upon his release, he came to New York City to speak at the United Nations.

I have heard that some retirees have trouble with figuring out what to do with all of the time that they now have on their hands. That was not the case with me. While everyone's heart was aflutter due to excitement about Mandela's release, mine was beating heavily for another reason. I found my second love–bowling. I found a league.

While I was knocking down pins, African Americans in Arts & Entertainment were bowling strikes too. Denzel Washington won the Academy Award for Best Supporting Actor in the movie, *Glory.*

A tremendous literary accomplishment, Charles R. Johnson won the 1990 National Book Award for his book, *Middle Passage.*

Advancing to the rank of Brigadier General in the US Air Force was Marcelite J. Harris.

President George H. W. Bush opened 1991 by signing the Civil Rights Act of 1991. While doing so, acting in his office as the Chairman of the Joint Chiefs of Staff, Colin Powell facilitated the logistical warfare in the Persian Gulf and in Desert Storm that eventually led to a US victory and freedom for the Kuwaiti people.

Anita Hill came to the forefront in the fight against sexual harassment in the workplace. Many Blacks were upset about this because her testimony came about at a time when the person that she was accusing, Clarence Thomas, was in confirmation hearings for his Supreme Court Justice nomination.

More disturbing news came as reports of egregious police brutality was captured on video of police officers beating Rodney King almost unrecognizably. The following year, in 1992, riots broke out all over Los Angeles when the police officers accused of the beating were acquitted of all charges. During the riots, fifty-two people were killed and there was an estimated five million dollars in property damage.

Before then, though, there were some good things that happened in our community. Frederick McKinley Jones was post-humously awarded the National Medal of Technology for his invention and patenting of over sixty useful devices involving food preservation and refrigeration.

In Arts and entertainment, Whoopi Goldberg won the Academy Award for Best Supporting Actress in the movie, *Ghost.* Also making an appearance at the Academy Awards was John Singleton. He became the first African American to be nominated for an Academy Award in the Best Director category for his film, *Boyz N the Hood.*

In sports, Earvin "Magic" Johnson announced his retirement from professional basketball due to his testing positive for the HIV virus.

In January of 1992, President William Jefferson Clinton was elected the 42nd President of the United States. He appointed his longtime friend and supporter, Vernon E. Jordan, as chairman of his transition team.

A victory for women and women of color, Carol Mosely Braun of Illinois became the first African American woman to be elected to the United States Senate.

Following her victory, 1992 saw sixteen new African Americans elected to Congress in the House of Representatives.

In 1993, President Clinton chose five African Americans to serve in his cabinet: Ronald Brown as Secretary of Commerce, Michael Espy as Secretary of Agriculture, Hazel O'Leary as Secretary of Energy, Jesse Brown as Secretary of Veteran Affairs and Joycelyn Elders as Surgeon General. I thought it important to mention their names and positions so that everyday people know who they are. They achieved great things and deserve to be recognized.

Also on the list of people who deserve to be recognized are Toni Morrison, for becoming the first African American to win the Nobel Prize for literature, and Thurgood Marshall. He died in January of 1993 but his legacy as a justice on the high court helped him to advance the civil liberties of all African Americans.

In sports, notable recognition went to Michael Jordan. After achieving remarkable achievements in the NBA, he retired from the Chicago Bulls.

We lost an angel in 1993. Clara "Mother" Hale, founder of Hale House in New York for drug addicted and HIV infected infants went home to be with the Lord on December 18, 1993.

Just as the Lord allowed the hate-filled man who killed the four girls in the church in Birmingham to be brought to justice and prosecuted, he did the same for the murderer of Medgar Evers, field secretary for the NAACP. After thirty years, Byron De La Beckwith was convicted of Evers' 1963 murder.

Four years after the release of Nelson Mandela, Black South Africans, for the first time, were allowed to cast their votes in an open election. The African National Congress and Nelson Mandela were both winners as he took office as President on May 10, 1994.

It was also in 1994 when the devil tried to take my life again. He couldn't get to me as a young man. He couldn't break me with Valerie's accident. He failed when I was in the hospital having neurosurgery. When none of those worked, he kept trying. In 1994, I was diagnosed with prostate cancer. Just to show him how much he really didn't have me, I didn't miss a week of bowling. My partners and I bowled every week without fail. I had 30 radiation treatments and didn't miss one week. As a matter of fact, I was bowling better than ever. I was bowling 200, 250, 270's…I even got a certificate. It was great.

It was not long after this that I met a man that changed my life, again. He was a salesman and he was selling a health product called *Noni* juice. He told me that it was a completely natural alternative medicine used for treating a wide variety of ailments like asthma, fever, constipation, eye problems, skin problems and others. I had been having so many problems with my eye, I decided to give it a try. I could barely see out of one eye at the time, so I was willing to try almost anything.

After I tried it for a little while, I saw a definite improvement in my vision and my energy levels. I continued to take it. As a matter of fact, I believed in the product so much, because of the results that I got, I became a salesman also. I even brought it to the church as a way that the church could have another stream of income.

With my newly improved vision, I could see that O.J. Simpson got more television time in 1995 than he may have gotten in his whole football career. It was in 1995 that he was acquitted in the long, highly charged trial where his ex-wife Nicole Brown and her friend Ronald Goldman were murdered. Blacks were especially excited about this verdict because they felt like it was vindication for the Rodney King trial where the officers were acquitted.

Under President Clinton's leadership, the jobless rate went down to 5.4% of the total U.S. population.

Recognized for his music genius at the young age of 74, George Walker became the first African American composer to win the Pulitzer Prize for music. His winning composition was *Lilacs for Soprano or Tenor and Orchestra* which was based on a poem by Walt Whitman.

Back on top of the list of people to watch in the film industry, Will Smith's *Independence Day* made $112 million in the first week of its showing.

Showcasing their extraordinary athletic ability, Michael Johnson, Dominique Dawes and Carl Lewis made big splashes at the Summer Olympics held in Atlanta, GA. Michael Johnson won two gold medals; Dominique Dawes, the first Black woman to win a gold medal in

Olympics in Gymnastics, won gold as a part of the team to become known as the 'Magnificent Seven'; Carl Lewis won two gold and one silver medal.

After being reelected to his second term as president in 1997, President William J. Clinton awarded the Medal of Honor to seven of the approximate one million African American soldiers who fought in World War II, but whose contributions were omitted. Only one of the seven was still alive to receive his award at the special ceremony held at the White House: Vernon J. Baker. The others: Edward A. Carter Jr., John R. Fox, Will F. James, Jr., Ruben Rivers, Charles L. Thomas, and George Watson were all awarded post-humously.

In sports, African American golfer, Tiger Woods, became the youngest golfer to ever win the Masters Tournament. While we celebrated him, we also celebrated the Fiftieth Anniversary of Jackie Robinson's entry into the Major Leagues.

In 1998, we lost Stokely Carmichael, a black activist who was extremely active in the 1960's Civil Rights movement. He died at age fifty-seven on November 15th.

Singer, Lauryn Hill, set a record in 1999 by becoming the first female to win five Grammy Awards.

In sports, Venus and Serena Williams, tennis sisters, played in the finals. On September 10, 1999, Serena won the U.S. Open Championship, becoming the first African American woman to win since Althea Gibson in 1957 and 1958.

9

A New Millenium:
2000 and Beyond

The population in 2000 was 281,421,906 with 5.8 million of those people being unemployed. The National Debt was $5,413,000 and the average salary equated to $13.37/hr. The average teacher's salary was $39,347 and minimum wage was $5.15. The life expectancy of males and females were 73.1 and 79.1, respectively.

In February of 2000, I joined Reid Temple A.M.E. Church. It was one of the best decisions that I'd made in a long time. My wife and daughters had already been there for four years before I came. Michelle was the first to attend a worship service and she had lots of good things to say about her time there. Michelle was visiting the church with her friend. My wife and other daughters had been visiting Bethel AME in Baltimore, but when they visited Reid Temple and heard Pastor Washington preach...the rest is history! And so my coming there just brought us together as a family. It was and is great. I'm surrounded by people who love me.

Shortly after I joined Reid, Pastor Washington appointed me to the Steward Board of the church. Initially I declined because I wanted to rest. I'd been so active in church, and with working so much, I just wanted to take things easy.

There was (and is) a noon-day Bible study for Seniors that takes place at the church every Wednesday. It was after one of the Bible studies that I was approached about making a contribution to a book that the church was publishing about finances. I contributed a piece that gave instructions about how to pay off debt. My contribution to the book was well received and it made me feel good because I like to help people.

Shortly thereafter, I reconsidered and decided to become a member of the Steward

Board. Reid Temple invested a lot into me, and I wanted to give back through my service.

So, that's how I planned to live after I retired–carefree. But all around me, things were shaking up. This is such a different time from the years when I was a young man. It's almost like we are living in two different Americas. When I was growing up I didn't have the same worries and concerns that people do now. I also didn't have the same kinds of technology, and I guess they all go together. But there are so many significant things that have happened in this decade that have changed the way that we live.

On September 11, 2001, a terrorist group called Al Qaeda hijacked four commercial airliners and crashed three of them–two into the World Trade Center in NYC, and one into the Pentagon in Washington, DC. Nearly 3,000 people were killed. As a result, the US declared an official War on Terrorism. I have experienced war in my days, but nothing like what we are into now with this war. There is so much controversy surrounding the war and its merit.

There were all sorts of changes in the structure of the family that were unheard of when I was growing up and raising my own family. The issue of what is called "gay rights" is prevalent in America now. People of the same sex want to get married and want the State governments to sanction and recognize their unions as lawful, providing them all the benefits that are afforded to men and women getting married. But that goes against God and the Word of God and I don't care how much things change, I am against that (I Corinthians 6:9).

Even the physical world as we have known it is changing. There is a phenomenon called Global warming that is a major issue now. This phenomenon is defined as the increase in the average temperature of the Earth's near-surface air and oceans since the mid-twentieth century and its projected continuation. Some speculate that global warming is partly responsible for the devastation of Hurricane Katrina.

On August 29, 2004, the Hurricane made landfall in New Orleans, LA. The city of New Orleans' levee system failed and the city went underwater. It stayed that way for weeks. Nearly 2,000 people were killed, hundreds of thousands were displaced and an estimated $75 billion in direct damages were assessed. It was and is the costliest natural disaster in US History.

I would have it said that many of the people that were displaced after Hurricane Katrina were Black. They were left without sufficient help and some are still, a few years later, not back on their feet. George W. Bush., the president at that time, received a lot of criticism because he failed to respond quickly enough to the needs of the victims of Hurricane Katrina.

Yet, with all of the negative things that were going on (genocide in Darfur, suicide bombers all over the world, kids going to school killing other kids and teachers) the world at large is still progressing and doing things that I never thought I would see in my lifetime.

In 2005, in France, a partial face transplant was performed. The following year, an Australian, Dr. Ian Frazer, developed a vaccine for cervical cancer. These are the advancements that encourage me. I know that soon enough they will develop a vaccine or a cure for all cancer. The Lord is going to give us the wisdom to figure these things out.

But of all of the things big and small that have happened, there is one event that overshadows them all- to me. There was a man in Chicago that was a Senator. He was doing his job well there. He had a wonderful family. His wife, Michelle, and their two daughters, Sasha and Malia, were well taken care of. He was a politician but there was no negativity surrounding his name. The climate in America changed and the people needed a change. We were coming up on election time and there was a need for America to go in a different direction than the one it'd been on for the last 8 years with the Bush Administration.

The Lord, just like he called Moses, called this Senator out of Chicago to the forefront of the world's eye. This young man is something else. He is poised and articulate. He is not uptight like some of the other politicians. His name is Barack Hussein Obama and the Lord raised him up to become the first African American President of the United States of America. It was one of the proudest days of my life.

I remember the entire campaign. I was very involved. I even sold t-shirts, key chains and buttons with his face on them. I never thought that I would see anything like that in my day, but the Lord allowed it to happen and He allowed me to see it.

By now there are probably hundreds of books written about him and his family and their journey to the White House. But I thought that this achievement was the best one to end this book with, as it seals everything that I have written thus far.

I want my life to be a testimony to others that God can raise up anyone to do His work. I want this book to be part of my legacy that helps young people know that through a dedicated life of service to God, education and hard work, that they can achieve things that no one ever thought possible.

I went from being a young boy with holes in my shoes who didn't read well, to a businessman sought out by people, both Black and White, for my expertise in starting and operating a successful business. A business that I grew, with the Lord's help, from the ground up, that fed and clothed my family and paid for my children to attend college. I went from working 18 hours a day on plantations for wealthy White families, to owning my own business and comfortably supporting my family. I had to participate in sit-ins and rallies. I was the victim of race crimes and other unspeakable activities.

But the Lord allowed it all because He knew that one day He was going to allow me to freely walk into Louis Charles Rabaut Jr. High School, my voting location, and be amongst the millions that would elect the first African American President of the United States of America, President Barack Hussein Obama.

This book is filled with lots of interesting stories and facts about my history and our collective history as African Americans. My 86 years on God's earth have taught me that our collective history as Black people, and my testimony are intrinsically linked. For that I say, "To God be praised for the things He has done!!!"

DILLAHUNT
DEVOTIONALS

DILLAHUNT DEVOTIONALS

"People love to talk but hate to listen. Listening is not merely not talking, though even that is beyond most of our powers; it means taking a vigorous, human interest in what is being told us. You can listen like a blank wall or like a splendid auditorium where every sound comes back fuller and richer."

~ Alice Duer Miller

The words that fill these Devotional pages are meant to prick your heart and bring you closer to God. I've been given the gift of long life and with it I have attained wisdom. I'm sharing a part of that with you in these pages. This is a part of my legacy.

~ Hezekiah Dillahunt, Sr.

ALWAYS GIVE GOD THANKS

"In a meeting with a banker about a business loan, he said, 'You should invest in some stock.' And to help you do that, we are going to give you $5,000 instead of the $3,000 you are asking for." I said, 'God, thank you! The Lord has favor on me.'"

Sometimes when we accomplish things it is easy to forget God. We attribute our good fortunes to our educations, bank accounts, credit scores, etc. When we need God, we cry out. But when God blesses us, sometimes we forget to give thanks.

The truth is that even if your education, bank account, credit score, etc. *was* a factor in your good fortune, it was the Lord who made it possible for you to have those things. Without the air in your lungs that the Lord provides, you couldn't have gone to school to get the education that allowed you to get the job that allowed you to pay your bills that allowed your credit score to be where it is. So, you owe God thanks for it all!!

Don't let another moment of this day go by without giving God the proper thanks for all the things that we take for granted everyday!!

What are you grateful to God for? And who are you going to share it with?

MAKING A FAST DOLLAR

"I had another customer who was involved in "numbers." He always carried around $300-$400 in his pocket. One day someone called to ask him for a ride. When he walked out of his house, he was shot and killed. Sometimes it doesn't pay to try to make a fast dollar."

There is an art to learning to how wait on God. Sometimes we take the easy or fast way out of difficult situations because we have not learned to be patient and wait for God to move. There is always a consequence for lack of patience. They say that good things come to those who wait. Unfortunately, for the numbers runner in my shop, the converse of that statement is also true.

As disciples, we should always be working on being more like Christ. To this end, spend some time today working on waiting. Be conscious of your disposition in the bank lines, or on hold for operators. Don't let your attitude sour when you find that something that you've been waiting on has still not come through. Little acts of discipline daily make for a stronger Christian.

GOD IS ALWAYS WORKING BEHIND THE SCENES

"While making plans to be married, my fiancée and I went to the American Security Bank to secure a loan to buy a house. I owned a well-kept 1954 Mercury that I had planned to use as additional collateral for the down payment, if necessary. The bank officer gave us the loan and never even looked at the car. It was the spring of 1958, and God was still working things out for me."

The Roman philosopher, Seneca, said that luck is where opportunity and preparation meet. As believers, we know that we don't need luck because we have God's favor. But that doesn't negate the fact that we have to be prepared to walk through the doors that the Lord opens for us. Begin preparing for the things that you believe God for. Start organizing and cleaning out the cluttered spaces of your life/mind. God is always working behind the scenes. So we have to do our part and be ready for the big show. Because I was prepared for God to move, He did.

WAIT ON THE LORD

"I really got kicked around when I decided to get into the oil business. When inquiring about buying a gas station, I first went to Sunoco Oil. That was where I had my first job. They turned me down. I went to Exxon, but was told that they had a waiting list a mile long. After much effort and waiting, Shell gave me a break. Two years after I opened my station, Exxon came and offered me the largest station on South Dakota Ave. I declined and stayed with Shell until I retired."

The Lord knows what is best for us. We just have to have the faith and patience to let His plan work in our lives. Perhaps the door that closed in your face was Him trying to guide you to the door that He wants you to walk through. He can use anyone, even your enemies to bless you. Practice looking for Him to do something miraculous today.

154

YOU'RE NEVER TOO YOUNG TO SERVE

"And you talking about poor. We were poor. Jesus said He came to see the poor. I know he came for me. When I was 12 years old, I decided that my mother and father's prayers would do me no good. I decided to make Jesus *my* choice."

There is an unspoken idea that being saved, and living for God is something that people do when they are older adults. Coupled with this notion is the idea that childhood and being young are the times to be spent being foolish, and doing your thing. Not so. The Lord doesn't discriminate. David and Samson are two of the most well-known figures in the Bible, and they were called to service as children.

Don't think that you are too young, too inexperienced, too anything, to be used by God. He is just looking for an open vessel. How can you make yourself more available for God?

YOU DESERVE RESPECT

I told my fiancée that I respected her for being a lady. I hoped that I could spend the rest of my life with her and that she would be the mother of my children.

Most music videos, rap songs, and hip hop magazines that are popular today portray women as sex objects and people who neither desire nor warrant respect. They are projected to the world with little or no clothing, posed in sexually provocative/suggestive manners and displayed so that men buying these magazines or watching these videos are aroused. It's about generating revenue, and the scantily clad backs and bottoms of women are apparently big business.

We are overdue for a return to purity. Today, reach out to your daughters and the other young women in and around your life and encourage them to say no to being treated like video vixens. Be the example of a woman that deserves and demands respect. Teach the young ones by word and deed, to value themselves for their intelligence and to walk in the attitude that *who* they are is not summed up in their physical beauty. There is a young generation that we have to win back, and it begins with one young man or woman at a time.

There is an African proverb that states "*it takes a village to raise a child*." The times that we live in are certainly indicative that we have strayed away from that way of living. But it's not too late to make a difference. Start today with telling one young woman that she is fearfully and wonderfully made. Take a child underneath your wing and groom them. Be a mentor. Find a way to give back to the community through the youth. If everyone reached out and began to teach, nurture and love, before long, we'd be a village once again.

DISCLOSURE

A lot of marriages end as a result of one party, or both, failing to disclose things about themselves before they get married. But, if a person loves you, they love *you*. That includes the parts of you that aren't so wonderful. If they love you, they will accept your past and work with you to create a better future. So, there is no need to alter yourself or hide parts of yourself to appear as anything or anyone other than who you really are. When God joins two people together, the real miracle, as evidenced by my 52-year union with my wife, is that He takes two imperfect people and brings them together to create love, which is always perfect in His eyes.

Is there a secret that you're keeping from someone you love?

PRAY WITHOUT CEASING

"I was taking some mechanics courses and having trouble figuring out how to repair a part in a car. I remembered a little sketch that I'd drawn and left in my Bible. I prayed and asked the Lord to show me how to fix the part and He did."

So often, when God blesses us with gifts we forget to continually pray and talk to God concerning them. In this example, I tried to show how we are to continually go to God concerning our gifts.

God doesn't have to do anything that He does for us. We cannot take any credit for anything that we are able to do with what He has given us. So, take some time each day and thank God for the gifts and talents that He has given you. Let Him know that you recognize that you are nothing and can do nothing without Him. Its only when you decrease, that the Lord is able to elevate and increase you and your territory.

159

A WISE MAN SEES EVIL AFAR OFF

"There was a girl that lived in my neighborhood. My sister picked her up and brought her to our house for my father's wake. They were sitting around for hours, like people do in the country. About 3 or 4 o'clock in the morning, she gets ready to go home. She didn't live far away, and it was very dark so I offered to take her home. When we got in the car, she said she didn't want to go home, but wanted to talk with me privately. While we were out, I yielded to temptation and slept with her."

Part of growing up and maturing as a Christian is learning what our temptations are, and steering clear of them. Oftentimes, when we find ourselves in a tempting situation, we are seemingly unable to resist because our "restraint muscles" have not been adequately exercised.

In the story, a young woman was my weakness. What is yours? Take some time and examine yourself. Pray and ask the Lord to reveal what your weaknesses are and how to overcome them. Then work on exercising restraint. Start with something small. Drink one less cup of coffee. Wake up 10 minutes earlier to better prepare for your day. In time, you'll find that the exercising of discipline in the smaller areas of your life will aid you in exercising discipline when the big challenges come

TRAIN UP YOUR CHILDREN IN THE WAY THEY SHOULD GO

"I've never been drunk. I didn't smoke. I didn't curse, but women were my downfall. I guess I took right after my daddy."

We need to be models of who we want our children to become. They are always watching, and we are always teaching. It's time-out for the "do as I say and not as I do" way of raising our children. If you smoke, it should be of no surprise to you to find cigarettes in your children's rooms. If you overeat, you shouldn't be surprised when the doctor tells you that your child is overweight. If you are sexually promiscuous, you shouldn't act as though you are surprised when your children can't be faithful to their partners. Jesus offers us a model of how we are to lead by example. Let's work on being more like Christ.

In what ways could you set a better example for your children, or the children that you have influence over? If you are a child, what are some of the things that you have been negatively influenced by that you saw an adult do? How can you overcome what you saw and do the Christ-like thing?

TO CONTACT THE AUTHOR

Hezekiah Dillahunt
hezekiahdillahunt@gmail.com
phone 202-679-2011

Please include your testimony or help received from
this book when you write.

Your prayer requests are also welcomed.

TO ORDER MORE BOOKS:
hezekiahdillahunt@gmail.com
www.anointedpresspublishers.com
www.amazon.com